Data Analytics

For

Absolute Beginners

A Deconstructed Guide to Data

Literacy

Second Edition

ISBN: 9781081762469

FIND US ON:

Monthly Newsletter

http://eepurl.com/gKjQij

Enjoy book recommendations, free giveaways of future book releases from the author, and other blog posts and news concerning machine learning, trends, and data science.

Teachable

www.scatterplotpress.com

For introductory video courses on machine learning as well as bonus video lessons included with this book.

Skillshare

www.skillshare.com/user/machinelearning_beginners

For introductory video courses on machine learning and video lessons from other instructors.

Instagram

machinelearning_beginners

For mini-lessons, book quotes, and more!

Table of Contents

Dedicated to broader data literacy in a fast-changing world

## 1

THE COLLECTION OF DATA

With its aptness to describe the past and predict our future, data has evolved into a store of value to hoard, trade, and even plunder. An upsurge in technology and mass digitalization means our universe is increasingly documented and data is the chosen format to chronicle this constant flux of information.

Data now circulates as electronically stored information, but data is not a new phenomenon or simply a recent uptick in the Information Age. While the equipment used to store, manage, and mine data consists of cutting-edge technology, today's servers and smart devices are simply the newest tools in a long line of evolutionary development.

Hunter-gathers collected data using tally marks etched into animal bones. Ancient civilizations (including the Egyptians and Sumerians) invented symbolic writing systems, large-scale surveys, counting devices, and even cryptography. (Similar to how companies encrypt their sensitive data today, artisans in Mesopotamia used cryptography to protect their secret recipes for pottery glaze.)

This innate human obsession with information gathering is consistent throughout history and has only heightened since the Scientific Revolution. Starting with the Copernican Revolution in 1543 and culminating in 1687 with Isaac Newton's "grand synthesis," the Scientific Revolution is notable for an acceleration of scientific discoveries beginning with Nicholas Copernicus dismissing Earth as the stationary center of the universe. Technological progress flourished during this period and by the time Isaac Newton published *Laws of Motion* (considered one of the most important works in the history of science), scientists in Europe were tinkering with electricity, the telescope, the microscope, calculus and logarithms, air pressure, and Blaise Pascal's mechanical calculator.

Using an arrangement of cogs that could quickly add and subtract large numbers, the calculator was an important innovation, but the device was also built on a number of breakthroughs before Pascal, including the Indo-Arabic numeral system, negative numbers, and the place value system.

Devised in Ancient Egypt in 3500 BC, the place value system was created to represent larger units and simplify arithmetic. Using the place value system, 151 could be expressed using seven symbols (1 hundred, 5 tens, and 1 unit) instead of 151 individual markings or symbols. Negative numbers, meanwhile, appeared in China, around 200 BC, as red and black rods to represent payments and debts in commercial transactions. Modern numerals originated in India in 100 BC and were quickly adopted by scholars in the Arab world. Europe's adoption of Indo-Arabic numbers came in the Middle Ages—just in time for Blaise Pascal and the Scientific Revolution.

While the Scientific Revolution profited from discoveries from the ancient world, rapid progress during this era radically changed how data was used. Deeper than an exercise in state bookkeeping, data collected in this period changed how the natural world was studied and understood. According to John Henry, a historian of the Scientific Revolution, detailed observations and investigatory experiments came to replace "reliance on ancient authority as the supreme source of knowledge" for interpreting the natural world.[1]

---

[1] John Henry, "The Scientific Revolution and the Origins of Modern Science," *Palgrave*, Third Edition, 2008.

Lawrence Principle in *The Scientific Revolution: A Very Short Introduction calls the* era "a busy laboratory of experimentation in all areas of thought and practice."[2] This included "a substantial increase in the number of people asking questions about the natural world, a proliferation of new answers to those questions, and development of new ways of gaining answers."[3] Rather than simply tallying peoples and lands, data provided the source code to radical new theories made by eminent figures including Copernicus, Galilei, Pascal, and Newton.

Evidence of the new emphasis on data for interpreting outside phenomena is seen in John Graunt's 1662 study on *Natural and Political Observations Made upon the Bills of Mortality*. Responding to a public health crisis in Europe, Graunt developed the first "life table" that surmised the probability of survival for a range of age groups. By analyzing the weekly bills of mortality (deaths), Graunt attempted to create a warning system to offset the spread of an epidemic plague in London. While the system was never implemented, Graunt's experiment in data processing divulged several interesting findings and served as a useful estimation of London's population.

After the Scientific Revolution, mechanical inventions carried the arrival of automated data processing, which gradually supplanted the heavy reliance on manual systems for data collection. Following the acceleration of new technology in the 20th Century, the word "data" (extracted from the Latin word "datum" or "that is given") also became increasingly associated with computers, and in 1946 its definition expanded to include "transmittable and storable computer information." "Data processing" appeared in the 1950s, and emanating from prolific developments in database storage, "big data" joined the lexicon in the 1990s.

---

[2] Lawrence Principle, "The Scientific Revolution: A Very Short Introduction," *Oxford University Press*, First Edition, 2011.
[3] Lawrence Principle, "The Scientific Revolution: A Very Short Introduction," *Oxford University Press*, First Edition, 2011.

While data has expanded beyond scientific circles to a daily ritual for the modern rank-and-file knowledge worker, true understanding (noted in this book as *data literacy*) lies in knowing what's behind the data. Everything from the data's source to the choice of independent variables and visual representation has consequences and sets the path from raw data to business insight. Like sending identical blocks of granite to stonemasons in different countries, data scientists can arrive at distinct viewpoints regarding the meaning and value of the same source data.

Part of the intricacy lies in the complexity of choices. Data practitioners operate in a complex market of methodologies, algorithms, and visualization options—not to mention software solutions, programming languages, and processing chips that affect how data is processed. Running a neural network on a GPU[4] cluster using the programming language C++ enables a data scientist to look at many more potential sample paths than running the language R on a CPU setup using the exact same data. Nor are patterns preordained to surface irrespective of the methods taken. Data literacy, therefore, necessitates a high-level understanding of data processing and thorough knowledge of how outputs are actually produced.

Decoding the data starts with knowing where the information came from and how it was collected. Given that anything recorded is data or a raw version of it, the full width of sources is difficult to capture in this chapter. Data takes the form of everything from words in books, to sales logged in spreadsheets, as well as text and images contained in social media posts. There's even data about data, called *metadata*, which describes information about data, such as the time of upload, duration, and tags of a video uploaded to YouTube.

---

[4] As a specialized parallel computing chip, a Graphics Processing Unit can perform many more floating-point operations per second than a Central Processing Unit.

To stay on course in our compact syllabus, we will focus on popular commercial channels of data collection including internal acquisition systems, data procurement, web scraping, alternative data, and open datasets.

Internal Acquisition Systems

The most common channel for data collection is internal acquisition. As the most reliable and accessible source of information, internal data is usually the first source an organization turns to for insight. Like turning out a sweater to reveal the inside stitching, internal records divulge the internal workings of an organization including relevant stakeholders, users, customers, suppliers, and partners.

Contemporary examples of internal systems include online signup forms, IoT device log records, web analytics software, and digital records of customer information stored in customer management systems (CMS). As moveable records of information, internal data is usually linked to a central database for storage. The data is also moveable inside the database and can be manipulated to return customized queries, exported as a CSV (Comma-Separated Values) file viewable in Microsoft Excel or imported into a separate analytics or visualization software program for analysis. In the case of massive amounts of data, data is stored across a network of computer servers using what's called a distributed file system.

In more recent times, the internal acquisition of data has become highly automated and linked to a feed of regular or instant inflows of information. The Very Large Telescope (VLT) in Chile, for instance, collects terabytes of data each night with its four telescopes Antu, Kueyen, Melipal, and Yepun. These telescopes, named after astronomical objects in the Mapuche language, service discoveries and track individual stars like those orbiting the Milky Way's supermassive black hole. Your own data acquisition, meanwhile, is probably closer to earth and runs 24 hours a day.

Internal data acquisition also represents an overhead to the organization, whether measured in dollars or time, and is an effort to set up and maintain. Thus, only when the value of internal data has been considered or exhausted, would an organization typically proceed to the next option of procuring data.

Data Procurement

While industry papers are quick to point out how organizations' technological ability to collect data outstrips their capacity to analyze it, this doesn't mean that the data we need is always available. A shortage of internal resources and constant demand for insight into the well-being of the organization can lead to gaps and shortages of appropriate data. In addition, organizations with negligent data collection procedures in the past might not have the internal data available to make informed decisions.

One method to fill internal gaps is to procure data from outside parties. This is the path Amazon took after closing a deal with AOL in the early 2000s. The sharing agreement allowed Amazon access to data from AOL's shopping channels, which Amazon used to train its own recommender system and pipe product recommendations to users.

As shown by Amazon, data can be procured under a sharing agreement or even purchased outright from a third party. If the data can't be bought or doesn't exist yet, then there's another paid option called *crowdsourcing*, which involves outsourcing tasks to a remote and distributed workforce. Amazon's Mechanical Turk (MTurk), for example, offers a marketplace for data-related tasks including data collection, deduplication, annotating datasets, training machine learning models, market research, cleaning and categorizing datasets, data validation, and more subjective tasks such as survey participation. Mechanical Turk differs from other gig-based marketplaces like Fiverr and Upwork because you can source contributions from hundreds or thousands of workers from one request, rather than negotiating with individual freelancers.

In 2018 I attended an event in Melbourne featuring the drag-and-drop design software Canva who shared with university students how they use Amazon's MTurk to outsource image preference surveys. With the company's two-person machine learning team unable to source data directly due to internal constraints, the company chose to source image preferences from virtual human respondents using Mechanical Turk. Canva then analyzed this data in-house to optimize the site's image suggestions to users.

Data validation is another task commonly outsourced to crowdsourcing platforms. The translation of a text into another language, for example, is a difficult task for in-house data science teams to verify, but a temporary workforce can help to verify translations as part of a data cleaning strategy. Automated tools like Google Translate, for example, are fast at translating search queries but tend to overlook the nuance of human errors, especially misspelled words and variants of key terms.

This problem is exemplified by search queries for the English football club Manchester City. While Google Trends indicates that "man city" is a common search query—higher in volume than "manchester city"—Google Translate doesn't always translate the true intent of the data input.

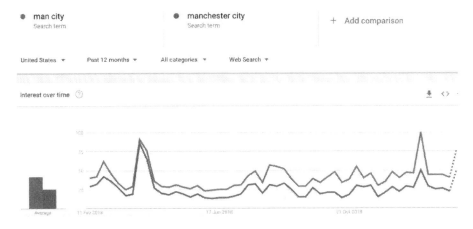

Figure 1: Google Trends' tracking of keyword search volume over the preceding 12 months with "man city" represented as the top line

Google Translate Results for "man city"

Chinese & Japanese: 男市 (the characters for "male" and "city")

French & German: man city

Italian: città dell'uomo

Spanish: hombre de ciudad

Of the above translations, only French and German are correct and were returned in English using no direct translation. As for amending the incorrect translations, this is a typical task for human help and an illustration of what the authors of *Human + Machine: Reimagining Work in the Age of AI* call the "missing middle." This term describes the fertile space where humans and machines collaborate to exploit the other's strengths.[5] Machines, for example, excel at managing large-scale repeatable tasks, while human expertise can help to maintain quality and provide feedback. Tools like MTurk make it convenient and cost-effective to link machine automation with human skills at scale.

---

[5] Paul R. Daugherty and H. James Wilson, "Human + Machine: Reimagining Work in the Age of AI," *Harvard Business Review Press*, 2018.

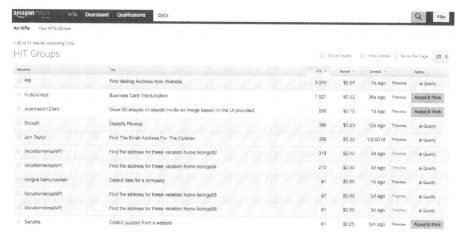

Figure 2: Example of the MTurk marketplace dashboard logged in as a Worker

If you're unsure about pricing projects on MTurk, it's important to set a price that values the time of the temporary worker. MTurk has separate interfaces for Workers and Requesters, so it's worth taking the extra 30 seconds to sign up and log into the Workers' dashboard to research the fee structure of similar projects advertised. This will help to maintain quality in your data returns.

Alternative Data

Well-known in the banking and finance world for feeding investment decisions, alternative data collates information gained and mined from non-traditional sources. In the case of investing, alternative data offers hedge fund managers and institutional investors information they can't find in regular sources like credit ratings. Non-traditional data sources include financial transactions, public records, SEC filings, press releases, social media monitoring, and online news articles. Once collected and consolidated, this information is mined to obtain unique and timely insight into a potential investment or business decision.

In the personal loans market, fintech companies in some countries use alternative data to overcome the absence of a formal individual credit rating. In China, for example, a country where up to approximately 60% of people have never owned a physical credit card and aren't eligible for credit with traditional banks, there are some finance providers who issue credit to customers based solely on the input of alternative data.[6] Alipay, for example, allows users to make credit-based purchases on e-commerce sites run by Alibaba based on the user's makeshift credit score, which includes the user's online spending habits. The company doesn't publicly disclose all the variables it collects and analyzes but common variables observed in this industry include the applicant's level of education, the frequency of data input corrections made during the signup process, purchasing and repayment history, and the credit score of the applicant's social contacts. Lenders in China are also vying for other personal information to feed credit scores, including records of cheating on the national university entrance examination and public transport convictions.

Given the rise of electronic data collection and the declining cost of mass data storage, there's a promising case for alternative data beyond personal loans and banking. In real estate, the Dutch startup Suburbia.io tracks gentrification—changes in neighborhoods that bring in wealthier residents, investment, and development—using non-traditional data sources. Their data points include satellite imagery, online Yelp reviews and listings, shipping receipts, and social media posts. Suburbia emphasizes the value of these real-time data points over traditional data such as census reports and migration analysis, which often contain time lags (between the point of collection to reporting) and extended gaps between reporting periods.

Other contemporary use cases for alternative data include precision agriculture, military monitoring, and influenza tracking. In the case of agriculture, farmers rely on drones to analyze

---

[6] Rebecca Fang, "Chinese Fintechs Use Big Data To Give Credit Scores To The 'Unscorable'", *Forbes*, July 25 2017, https://www.forbes.com/sites/rebeccafeng/2017/07/25/chinese-fintechs-use-big-data-to-give-credit-scores-to-the-unscorable/#7bc35736410a

time-series images of crops to improve crop management and yield predictions.

While alternative data can be expensive to produce, a large amount of alternative data is open data (that is publicly available), including Google Maps and Yelp restaurant reviews. In some cases, the holder of the data doesn't recognize its secondary value and undervalues it or releases it for free. However, this is not to say that free data is a cheap source of business insight. The complexity of compiling hundreds of disorganized data sources makes it difficult to store, manage and analyze alternative data using traditional software (i.e. relational database management systems and Microsoft Excel). This has led to a quiet breakout in alternative data providers charging premium fees to corporate clients. For a list of vendors, see alternativedata.org and their verified list of alternative data providers at https://alternativedata.org/verified-list-of-alternative-data-providers/.

Web Scraping

The best way to source public data—and potentially alternative data—is *web scraping*. This time-honored technique involves collecting information from the web using code and automation; saving the hassle of clicking through a large number of web pages and manually copying and pasting information into a spreadsheet.

Web scraping has valuable commercial applications for search engine companies including Google, Yahoo, and Baidu who use scraping to crawl and index millions of web pages. Other companies use web scraping to aggregate information and offer side-by-side price comparisons, such as hotels, flights, and other booking services.

The go-to programming language for web scraping is Python, and basic programs that automatically export information into a CSV file can be written in less than 40 lines of code. A good place to learn web scraping is online tutorials teaching Python and

Beautifulsoup (a Python programming package that simplifies the code for scraping websites).

There are also online tools available that make scraping a simple drag-and-drop job for non-programmers. A popular tool is Import.io, which is a browser tool you can use to scrape information from the web in three easy steps.

1) Download: Use the web browser tool to download information from a web server to load and display.

2) Parse: Extract useful segments of information based on defined guidelines using a technique called parsing that analyzes the text as logical syntactic components. For instance, the tool can be configured to scrape Twitter posts and comments but avoid information such as menu items and the website footer.

3) Store: Take the scraped data and store it on Import.io or export the data to your cloud storage platform or as a file type such as JSON (JavaScript Object Notation) or CSV (Comma-Separated Values).

Import.io is a fee-for-service tool but they offer a free trial option and you can request free access if you are a student, teacher, journalist, charity, or startup. You can learn more about how to use this tool on your own or by joining this video course on Udemy: Web Scraping for Sales & Growth Hacking with Import.io.

Open Data

If web scraping doesn't pique your interest, then an even quicker way to access relevant data is to download *open data*. This is data that can be freely used and shared by anyone for any purpose. Public datasets are available on a number of platforms including government agency websites (i.e. data.gov and ukdataservice.ac.uk), Google Cloud's Public Dataset program, Microsoft Research Open Data, World Bank Open Data, and, of course, Kaggle.com.

As an organized online community for data scientists and statisticians, Kaggle.com hosts an impressive library of open datasets. Datasets on the site are uploaded by members of the community or submitted by companies as part of open data competitions. A good portion of these datasets contain data collected from the real world, including Starbucks' sales data and online movie ratings. You can also find artificial datasets, which are great for beginners, as they are usually well-organized and ready for immediate use—saving the issue of dealing with messy data and missing values.

Compliance

Whether you choose to scrape the Internet for alternative data or extract data directly from your customers, it's crucial to operate in compliance with contemporary data laws. As noted in *Data Leverage: Unlocking the Surprising Growth of Data Partnerships* authored by brothers Christian and James Ward, "for many, data assets are an afterthought to normal business operations"[7] and compliance is commonly overlooked.

An O'Reilly Media survey conducted in June 2018[8] revealed that only one in two (53%) respondents from companies with extensive experience in machine learning check data for privacy issues and 43% of respondents among all companies.[9]

Part of the reason for this attention gap is the lag and lack of industry standards. As Robert Langkjær-Bain argues, "we are very much in the early days" of data compliance and this space remains an active area for researchers.[10] Academic researchers are currently writing papers that are being translated into best

---

[7] Christian J. Ward & James J. Ward, "Data Leverage: Unlocking the Surprising Growth of Data Partnerships," *Ward PLLC*, 2019.
[8] The survey was sent to past attendees of O'Reilly Media's Strata Data and/or AI Conferences as well as those who have previously consumed online content produced by O'Reilly Media. Respondents were from North America (6,000+), Europe (2,000), and Asia (1,700+).
[9] Ben Lorico & Paco Nathan, "The State of Machine Learning Adoption in the Enterprise," *O'Reilly Media*, 2019.
[10] Robert Langkjær-Bain, "Data Rights and Wrongs," *Significance Magazine*, December 2018 Issue.

practices and checklists for industry practitioners and working with industry to organize relevant conferences.[11]

For now, data transparency—sharing how you collect data—is the first step in meeting compliance requirements. Many of the class-action lawsuits made in California against Wal-Mart, Crate & Barrel, Victoria's Secret, Target and other retailers didn't follow this first step of acting with transparency. This included mining customers' zip code information when completing a credit card transaction.[12]

Procuring data can also lead to legal problems, especially with the prevalence of intermediaries peddling personal data, including users' political affiliation and health status, and the inherent difficulty of distinguishing how these details were collected. The company Rapleaf, for instance, was exposed in 2010 by a Wall Street Journal investigation that found the company was violating both Facebook and MySpace's terms of service by selling identifiable user details.

This incident also came a year after a woman in America's Midwest sued Netflix for disclosing her sexual preferences as part of the 2007 Netflix Prize dataset. Despite Netflix's best attempt to remove personal identifiers from the data, including the names of individuals, personal identities were later revealed by matching the competition's dataset with film ratings from the publicly available Internet Movie Database. Researchers from the University of Texas found that an anonymous user's rating of six obscure movies could be used to identify an individual Netflix user with an 84% success rate.[13] Netflix lost the resulting legal case and was pressured to cancel its second open data competition.

---

[11] Robert Langkjær-Bain, "Data Rights and Wrongs," *Significance Magazine*, December 2018 Issue.

[12] Some of these appeals were successfully taken to the Supreme Court for using pretenses to deduce customer mailing addresses (by linking the customer's name and zip code).

[13] Viktor Mayer-Schonberger & Kenneth Cukier, "Big Data: A Revolution That Will Transform How We Live, Work and Think," *Hodder & Stoughton*, 2013.

For data science teams, it's important to work closely with legal experts and advisors to avoid these issues and act transparently regarding how data is used and collected. This can be a delicate balancing act, but as Christian and James Ward point out, failure to behave with transparency is the number one cause of lawsuits.

## 2

STORING DATA

Data storage is a USD $56.8 billion market and navigating the many different storage options starts with understanding the make-up of your data.[14] Size and composition have a major bearing on where and how your data is stored. Data measured in petabytes can be hosted on the cloud as part of a distributed data storage solution, while smaller quantities can be stored in a centralized location that's fast and easy to access, such as a relational database management system. Other popular forms of data storage include key-value stores and data warehouses. Structured data, unstructured data, and big data also demand their own specific storage needs as we'll cover later in this chapter.

We first need to discuss *raw data*—because all information starts, at least initially, as raw data. This is data that's been collected but is yet to be manipulated or processed. Like crude oil extracted from the earth's crust, raw data is sorted and refined before it's sent down the pipeline for processing and value extraction. To put this process into perspective, let's examine the following sample of raw data.

---

[14] "The next-generation data storage market is estimated to grow from USD 56.8 billion by 2019 to USD 102.2 billion by 2024 at a CAGR of 12.48%," *MarketWatch*, April 8 2019, https://www.marketwatch.com/press-release/the-next-generation-data-storage-market-is-estimated-to-grow-from-usd-568-billion-by-2019-to-usd-1022-billion-by-2024-at-a-cagr-of-1248-2019-04-08

On the 15th of December, 2013, Dodie Egolf uploaded his project "Nail Art and Photos Printed on your Nails w/ Embellishments" to the website Kickstarter.com, the world's largest crowd-funding platform for creative projects. The project attracted a total of six pledges from the Kickstarter community but failed to reach its target of USD $20,000 in funding.

In its present form, we can't analyze this data using quantitative methods because the key information contained in the text is yet to be organized and formatted. Most general-use algorithms accept only numeric or categorical data as input—and not raw blobs of text. However, embedded in this paragraph is a rich array of valuable information including the date, creator, name, number of pledges, target, and outcome of a Kickstarter campaign. By extracting these six features and using the rows and columns of a tabular dataset to store those values, we can convert the raw data into *structured data*, which is more convenient for processing.

Structured Data

Structured data describes information organized into a format that is well-defined and easy for algorithms to retrieve and process critical information. In order to be quickly retrieved, the information is arranged and organized into fixed fields that define the format, variable type, and the maximum or expected size.

The rows and columns of a relational database or tabular spreadsheet (as shown in Table 1) are a common format for storing structured data.

Campaign_Name	Date
Nail Art and Photos Printed on your Nails w/ Embellishments	15/12/2013

Table 1: Date of a Kickstarter campaign contained in a tabular dataset

The top row, marked in black, represents the table's header and describes the contents of the row(s) below. The table has two columns, each containing an individual feature. In the case of the left column, Nail Art and Photos Printed on your Nails w/ Embellishments have been added to denote the item documented. By searching the relevant feature column and the row of the corresponding item, we can add the next item of information, which is the date of the Kickstarter campaign. To better process this value, we can convert the raw data (15th of December, 2013) into a standard format used for recording dates. At the same time, we can add horizontal columns to store the values of the other four features: Creator, Pledges, Target, and Outcome shown in Table 2.

Campaign_Name	Date	Creator	Pledges	Target_USD	Outcome
Nail Art and Photos Printed on your Nails w/ Embellishments	15/12/2013	Dodie Egolf	6	20000	Failed

Table 2: All six features of the Kickstarter campaign

Each column now contains an individual feature, i.e. Date, Creator, Pledges, Target_USD, and Outcome, with relevant values stored in the corresponding cells below. In data science terminology, multiple columns/features are referred to as *matrices* or an *array*.

Minor adjustments have also been made to prepare the data for processing. This includes transforming the format of the date and the removal of the comma and dollar symbol for the value "$20,000." Commas aid human eyes to read large numbers, but such niceties aren't necessary, or even supported, by computer programming language. The currency symbol has also been removed as, again, it's not necessary for computer processing.

The currency has instead been added to the column header for human reference.

We have now converted the raw data into processable information. Let's next add two additional campaigns to the dataset.

Campaign_Name	Date	Creator	Pledgers	Target_USD	Outcome
Nail Art and Photos Printed on your Nails w/ Embellishments	15/12/2013	Dodie Egolf	6	20000	Failed
Grippity: World's first Transparent Tablet	15/12/2013	Jacob Eichbaum	212	199000	Failed
Bike Thief's Debut Album "Blessed Are the Sleepy Ones"	15/12/2013	Bike Thief	114	7000	Successful

Table 3: Expanded dataset with three items

With the addition of two new rows, the table has expanded vertically, and each row below the header describes an individual Kickstarter campaign according to six separate features.

With additional data contained in the two new rows, we're ready to perform basic analysis to summarize the data, such as:

1) Calculate the average success rate of projects (Successful Outcomes/Total Outcomes, 1/3 = 33.33%)
2) Tally the number of Pledgers (Sum of Pledgers = 332)
3) Generate a ratio of Pledgers to Target funding (Pledgers:Target, 332:226000)

Unstructured Data

Unlike structured data, unstructured data consists of information that isn't organized in a discernible way and doesn't fit into a standard structure like a tabular dataset. This type of data is often text-heavy and comes in many mediums, including images, videos, PDF files, email messages, satellite images, and audio recordings.

Although these records of information hold many of the same valuable features as structured data, the structure of the data makes it difficult for machine models to retrieve, analyze, and process. General algorithms aren't capable of combing a two-hour film for the name of the protagonist. (Note that the metadata about the movie, i.e. name of the director, year of release, genre, protagonists, etc., qualifies as structured data. Metadata is abstracted from the data and sits above unstructured and structured data to provide a "larger picture" of what's taking place below and can be stored and analyzed separately just like structured data.)

Unstructured data calls for alternative forms of storage, sometimes referred to as data lakes—a dumping ground for unconventional data. Specific examples include key-value stores, object-based storage, and Hadoop (distributed file system).

Finally, it's important to acknowledge that data isn't wed to one category. Non-structured data can be transformed into structured data using extraction techniques that port features into fixed fields. Likewise, raw data can be rearranged as structured or unstructured data. Thus, rather than pigeonhole email data as unstructured data and sales data as structured data, it's important to consider data categories as liquid information assets that can transform under the supervision of the database's architect.

In addition, what we describe as raw data and unstructured data is relative and context-specific. For an email message, we might use a technique from natural language processing (NLP) called *stemming* to normalize the text by reducing words to their original stem, i.e. "connectivity," "connected," "connections" > "connect." In addition, we might drop stop words from the text like "the," "is," and "are." The data is still unstructured but in the context of natural language processing, the data is ready for processing and is no longer raw data. Thus, what some data scientists view as raw data might constitute unstructured data (ready for processing) for another. Practitioners working in NLP, for instance, generally have a different threshold for what they view as raw data than those working in data mining searching for statistical correlation.

Finally, there is *semi-structured data*, which is data that fails to conform with the standard models of storage for structured data but contains tags or other labels that separate semantic elements, thereby providing a hierarchy of fields within the data. Email messages and XML (Extensible Markup Language) are both examples of semi-structured data.

Big Data

Dramatic developments in computer processing power, storage, and automated systems to collect data have led to massive reserves of data called *big data*. While the value of data to organizations and businesses at large has grown steadily over the past two decades, what constitutes big data remains hard to define. When it was coined in 1997, the term "big data" was used as an adjective to describe a "big data problem" rather than to quantify the size of data.

The classification of big data is also relative to technology. What's considered "big" and computationally expensive to process today might not hold true for another computer system in the future. As Moore's Law predicts that physical capacity and computer performance double nearly every two years, there's no agreed threshold for qualifying big data in terms of rows and columns or size. The most accepted definition of big data is large amounts of information that defy conventional methods of processing.

Another well-accepted benchmark for qualifying "big data" is the three V's Gartner analyst Doug Laney termed in 2001. In his research publication *3D data management: Controlling data volume, variety and velocity*, Laney proposed characterizing big data by volume, velocity, and variety. The first of the three V's, "volume," refers to the capacity of machines to stockpile near-incomprehensible quantities of data. Initially, at least, volume was the primary metric for describing big data. Volume, though, was soon complemented by other considerations including variety and velocity that challenged conventional methods of storage and computer processing.

The next V, "variety," describes data that doesn't fit into a standard format like the rows and columns of a relational database or Excel spreadsheet. The variety of data might require storing data in multiple locations using different formats, which is a common method of storing unstructured data, such as images, audio, satellite images, and other media formats. In the case of locating a missing airplane or sea-going vessel, data is collected from multiple sources in various formats by satellites, ships, and navigation systems. The raw data is then consolidated to gain a clear picture of what transpired as well as clues for missing debris.

Lastly, "velocity" describes situations where data is generated at a fast tempo and has a relatively consistent structure (low variety) that maximizes portability. High-velocity data also goes by the name of "streamed data" and isn't necessarily stored, especially if it's used for monitoring and anomaly detection such as emergency detection systems.

Streamed data is difficult to analyze as the model must constantly update and respond to the influx of more data. In the case of analyzing Kickstarter campaigns, this would comprise processing and analyzing patterns while new data (including pledges and pledgers) updates every few seconds based on live activity.

In addition to the original three V's, "value" and "veracity" are often referred to as the fourth and fifth V's, serving as later additions made by the big data community. "Value" describes data that holds significance from a business/decision-making perspective, and "veracity" is the quality of the data, i.e. clean and accurate. Data collected from social media versus a government website (.gov) is a factor to consider when judging the value of your data.

Big data doesn't necessarily need to possess three or more V's to qualify as big data; one of the three primary V's advocated by Laney could be sufficient to cancel out a standard approach to data analysis.

Having consolidated the characteristics of structured data, unstructured data, and big data, we can now take a closer look at common storage solutions.

Relational Database Management Systems

A Relational Database Management System (RDMS) is a software program used to store structured data in multiple separate and interrelated tables, each resembling a standard spreadsheet. These systems were invented in the 1950s to succeed static spreadsheets for storing and retrieving data. Before RDMS, it was impractical to access and probe data from a single spreadsheet with up to a million rows displayed on a black-and-white terminal. By connecting multiple tables and customizing how the data was presented through the display window, RDMS made it easier to store and access structured data.

Data stored in tables is easy to retrieve as each table (also called a *relation*) contains data categories in columns. Each row contains a single instance of data according to the feature defined by the column. Additional tables then store further information specifying orders, products, suppliers, etc. The information contained in these tables interacts and is linked by key variables such as name or product ID, allowing the database manager to view or create a custom report drawn from multiple tables, i.e. customers that purchased certain products over a set time period. This means that data for one case (i.e. a customer or product) can be contained in multiple separate tables.

Efficiency is also a central advantage of using a relational database as multiple records can draw on the same information and a data input never needs to be entered more than once.

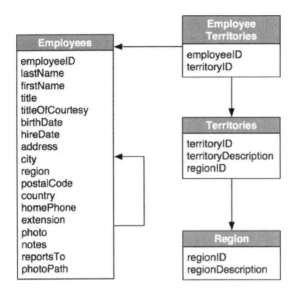

Figure 3: Example of a relational database

To organize and assign information, relational database systems rely on what's called a *schema*. These are rules that define what your data looks like and where it can be placed inside the relational database. A schema requires considerable upfront design from a database architect to determine the format and category of stored data. Most relational database management systems also use Structured Query Language (SQL) to access the stored data. Developed by IBM in the early 1970s, SQL is useful for handling data relationships including performing commands to manipulate and view data across multiple tables.

RDMS are still widely used today and especially for data warehousing, or what's known as an *Enterprise Data Warehouse (EDW)*.

Data Warehousing/Enterprise Data Warehouse

An enterprise data warehouse (EDW) is a relational database optimized to store data for the explicit purpose of post-analysis. The data warehouse is physically/virtually and functionally separate from the main database management system used for everyday operations and transactions.

The data warehouse is reserved for creating specific or enterprise-wide reports that support decision-making by offering consolidated and timely knowledge about the organization. These reports are used to improve business efficiency, sales, and marketing targets, customer service, or other functions. Collating relevant and up-to-date information, however, usually represents a significant investment of time and effort.

The data warehouse draws its data from relevant sections of the organization's database management system. Using programming scripts, ETL is often updated automatically on a daily or regular basis. The EDW's data is generally structured and pulled internally from other relational databases but it can also be unstructured too. Following a process known as Extract, Transform, and Load (ETL), data is extracted from numerous sources, transformed under a specified schema, and loaded into the data warehouse.

With data contextualized by key dimensions such as customer, time of purchase, and location, database practitioners can then conduct analysis and create reports under a system called Online Analytical Processing (OLAP). OLAP is different from Online Transaction Processing (OLTP), which involves storing data and processing it in real-time to implement non-analytical tasks (read-only), such as using SQL to retrieve information to prepare a purchasing order. E-commerce sites, for instance, need access to multiple tables of data to process requests, including customer billing information, mailing address, and information about current inventory levels. Rather than crank up a server and wait minutes to retrieve the data needed to process an order, SQL is used to instantly access that information and perform Online Transaction Processing.

The role of Online Analytical Processing is to then conduct a post-analysis of the data and provide a consolidated view of the organization. This might involve analyzing profitable areas of the business and geographical growth areas for new customers. New insights from OLAP can then be added to a regular reporting sequence or an interactive dashboard to share new business insights and help the enterprise track key metrics.

Key-Value Store

More than 80 percent of enterprise information today resides as unstructured data and key-value stores are an ideal storage system for this type of data.

Simple and easy to use, a key-value store is a database that stores data as a key-value pair. The key is marked by a string such as a filename, URI or hash, and matches a value, which can be any type of data such as an image or text document. Unlike a relational database, the value (data) doesn't require a schema definition and can be stored as a blob. This makes it fast to store, retrieve, and delete data. The downside is that because the value is vague, you can't filter or control what's returned from a request.

A popular key-value store solution is Apache Cassandra, which stores NoSQL without the need for schema or the use of SQL. As a free open-source distributed database management system, it's similar to Hadoop but serves as a key-value store. Apache Cassandra is ideal for handling massive amounts of data, such as indexing every web page on the Internet or serving as a backup system to replace tape recordings.

Distributed File Systems

As a recent solution for storing large volumes of data, distributed filing systems host data across a network of connected servers, known as nodes. Unlike relational databases and traditional key-value systems that host data on a single server, distributed filing systems are designed to scale across servers while still providing users access to data hosted across multiple nodes in the network.

The concept took root in the early 2000s and accelerated as a result of a research paper published in 2003 by Google launching the company's Google File System. After the paper came out, Dug Cutting and Mike Cafarella from Yahoo developed an open-source distributed filing system to store and analyze semi-structured and unstructured data. Named after the soft toy elephant of Cutting's son, Hadoop has become synchronous with distributed file sharing and is used by Facebook, eBay, Twitter, and many other tech companies to host large amounts of data.

Using Hadoop, data can be reliably stored and processed across hundreds or thousands of servers (nodes) located in data centers around the globe. The advantages of this storage method include the low cost of storage and adding servers, the ability to store data that doesn't have an explicit use in its original format, and the capacity to process chunks of data across servers simultaneously by splitting tasks across the network.

Cloud Solutions

To conclude this chapter, it's important to talk about the specific infrastructure employed to store data and the recent trends reshaping data management. The infrastructure for storing digitalized data can be split into traditional hardware and virtual resources. Traditional hardware is stored on-premise in the form of physical servers and storage devices—familiar to most people as the frenzy of cables and humming boxes set up inside secure rooms in schools and offices before the cloud era.

Starting with the evolution of Amazon Web Services (AWS) over a decade ago, cloud infrastructure in the form of virtual servers and databases has gradually replaced the large majority of these physical systems. Similar to how we consume and pay for electricity, gas, water, and traditional utilities, cloud computing provides flexibility to consume computational and storage resources based on actual needs. By using data infrastructure services available on the cloud, organizations avoid the upfront cost of provisioning physical hardware as well as the hefty cost to maintain, store, and upgrade that equipment. Users simply rent computing resources from a cloud provider in the form of virtual machines. This doesn't mean the machine is invisible or intangible; the server/machine is owned and managed by a cloud provider and stored inside a large data center. Users can access the machine over the Internet at any time to make modifications to their infrastructure, run applications or host a database.

From a data scientist's perspective, cloud technology helps to free up time to focus on analyzing data rather than configuring and maintaining intricate hardware. A full spectrum of tools, from visualized dashboards to powerful data processing chips, is available on-demand on a pay-as-you-go basis. In addition to cloud-based storage products such as RDMS, key-value stores, and distributed file systems, data scientists can access a range of powerful data processing chips, data migration tools, data streaming solutions, visualization tools, and data analytics as a service.[15] These products are mostly moving towards a drag-and-drop interface that makes both setup and programming dramatically easier. Lastly, the ability to access these product offerings from the same user account saves the hassle of exporting and importing massive datasets onto a different server and you can simply rent processing capacity when you need it using additional CPUs or GPUs.

---

[15] Examples include Microsoft Azure ML, Amazon Machine Learning, Google AutoML, and IBM Watson Analytics.

## 3

VARIABLES

Data is said to be the "new oil" of the world economy and while Google and Facebook look like the new oil barons and there's always the danger of an unintended leak, this is more of a marketing campaign than a true analogy.

Oil is a finite resource. It doesn't grow exponentially in a short space of time—nor is there a "big oil problem" in the sense of possessing too much oil. Secondly, as author Bernard Marrs has written for *Forbes*, oil loses its energy as heat or is permanently converted to another form such as plastic.[16] Data, meanwhile, is increasingly useful the more it's processed and consumed. Thirdly, the value of data is determined by the individual beholder and not spot pricing or the going rate of a global benchmark in the form of a commodity.

In many ways, the intrinsic value of data is closer to money. Just as the North Korean Won has limited value to consumers in North America, non-structured data is virtually useless to companies without the right infrastructure and expertise to store and analyze unconventional data.

Reminiscent of money, the maximum value that can be derived from business data is relatively short-term.[17] This is because the value of data typically depreciates over time, i.e. user contact

---

[16] Bernard Marrs, "Here's Why Data Is Not The New Oil," *Forbes*, March 5 2018.
[17] In some cases, the value of data can appreciate, i.e. historical and anthropological records such as the Rosetta stone and ancient clay tablets.

information, combinations of item purchases, and user behavior on old devices (i.e. blackberry and iPhone 1).

Like money, data also multiplies over time, and similar to printing too much money, there is a ceiling limit where too much data leads to problems including storage cost and noise. (The term "noise" is used to describe random and/or useless information that obscures the key meaning of the data.)

The analogy between money and data also fades, though, when we look at their specific functions. While both are considered an asset to store and hold value, money serves as a means of exchange whereas data serves as a record of knowledge. The other striking difference is how we perceive money and data. Divided into a fixed set of denominations, money manifests in the familiarity of copper, zinc, and nickel coins, and the flamboyant design of currency notes. These physical denominations make money tangible and easy for people to visualize and touch—less so for data. While data can be physical, it's much harder to name and recognize its many denominations.

Aside from structured, unstructured, and semi-structured categories, data falls into a finer taxonomy of denominations called *variables*. Like learning how supply and demand forces set the value of money, it is variables that enable us to understand, examine, and identify the value of our data.

Customer
Customer 1
Customer 2
Customer 3
Customer 4

Table 4: Data objects

Variables help to distinguish contrasting qualities between data objects, such as age, gender, and height. Data objects, meanwhile, are the items you are describing, such as products, customers, or films, and may also be referred to as *instances*, *data points,* or *samples*.

Customer	Age	Gender	Height_cm
Customer 1	28	Female	160
Customer 2	30	Female	172
Customer 3	33	Male	174
Customer 4	27	Female	159

Table 5: Data objects described by three variables

Variables are also known interchangeably as *features*, *dimensions* or *attributes*. In terms of usage, *feature* is commonly used in machine learning, *dimension* in data warehousing, *attribute* in data mining, and *variable* in statistics.[18]

In the context of computer science, the role of a variable is to label and store items of information in the machine's memory for later utilization. But from a data science perspective, variables are not only a container to hold information but measurables that vary in volume or type and share relationships with other variables, such as *independent* and *dependent variables.*

Independent and Dependent Variables

While there are three types of variables used in scientific experiments (independent, dependent, and controlled), in data science, analysis is limited to dependent and independent variables.

An independent variable (expressed as an uppercase "X" in data science notation) is the variable that supposedly impacts the dependent variable (expressed as a lowercase "y"). As you

---

[18] Jiawei Han, Micheline Kamber & Jian Pei, "Data Mining: Concepts and Techniques (The Morgan Kaufmann Series in Data Management Systems)," *Morgan Kauffmann,* 3rd Edition, 2011.

modify the independent variable, the effect on the dependent variable is observed and recorded. The size of someone's house (X), for example, tends to impact the monetary value of the house (y). Understanding the relationship between a dependent variable and its independent variable(s) enables you to predict patterns and take action, such as installing a second bathroom (X) to raise the value of your house (y).

In data analytics, the independent variables act as input and the dependent variable as the output. After the machine deciphers the rules and patterns between X and y, it creates what is known as a model: an algorithmic equation for producing an output (dependent variable) with new data (independent variables) based on the underlying trends and rules learned from the data. Other models, though, may only analyze independent variables before outputting a new dependent variable (discussed in Chapter 5 under *Data Mining and Unsupervised Learning*).

Independent and dependent variables can also be described by another sub-tier of qualities, including numeric, categorical, Boolean, and TimeDate variables.

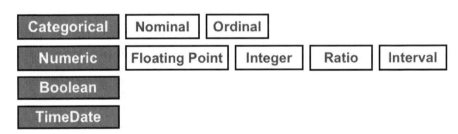

Figure 4: Common variable types

Numeric Variables

Numeric variables are expressed and processed mathematically on a numeric scale. There are two main types of numeric variables, *integer* and *floating-point numbers*. Integers are whole numbers, i.e. 7, 77, and 77, and floating-point are numbers with a decimal point, i.e. 7.7, 77.0, and 0.7. Percentages can also be described using floating-point numbers, i.e. 0.5 = 50%.

In addition to integer and floating-point numbers, there is the *ratio* variable which compares two items numerically, i.e. measuring the numeric ratio of data scientists to the number of employees (4:50). Another example is interval variables, which hold equally spaced intervals between values, i.e. $80,000, $90,000, and $100,000 (describing brackets of annual income). It's a requirement that the values are separated evenly by a fixed interval, such as units of 10,000.

TimeDate

TimeDate variables are simple to grasp because they are just that—records of time and date expressed in a string format, i.e. 2019-02-03. They can also vary in their specificity, including hours and seconds. Timestamps are the most common example of a TimeDate variable.

Categorical

Categorical variables, also known as *nominal variables,* are names or symbols of objects, such as a user's country of residence or the genre of a film (i.e. horror, action, or comedy). Nominal comes from the Latin word for "name" and is defined in English as "relating to or consisting of names."

For the most part, categorical/nominal variables are qualitative in nature and cannot be aggregated. While categorical variables are often expressed as strings of letters, it's possible to assign integers to categories, such as 0 = Male, and 1 = Female. While numeric notation aids the computer's ability to read and parse categories, these numbers are arbitrary and do not carry mathematical meaning that would facilitate aggregation or quantitative analysis. A male, for instance, cannot be aggregated with a female to generate a value of 0.5. Instead, these numbers are discrete and cannot be merged. Similarly, computing the average number of legs across animal species would be meaningless as two and four-legged animals are two discrete categories and cannot be aggregated to produce a mean of three.

Animals with two legs are assigned to one category and animals with four legs to another, thereby making these values discrete.

A special subcategory of categorical variables is ordinal variables, which categorize values in a precise and meaningful sequence. Unlike nominal variables, such as gender or film genre, ordinal variables contain an intrinsic ordering or sequence.

Examples of ordinal variables are:

1) low, medium, high
2) rookie, professional, expert
3) pre-undergraduate, undergraduate, postgraduate
4) 1-star, 2-stars, 3-stars, 4-stars, 5-stars
5) dissatisfied, neutral, satisfied, very satisfied

As can be elicited from these five examples, the ordering of values serves a logical purpose; "medium" is between "low" and "high," and "postgraduate" is the highest level of categorization presented in example three. Unlike interval variables that contain even intervals between values, the scale of separation between ordinal variables does not need to be consistent. Although there's a different margin between "rookie and professional" and "professional and expert," the margin of difference isn't considered important. Likewise, the margin between a three-star and a four-star review might be different from a one-star and a two-star review. If given the option, one-star reviewers might actually rate something less than one-star, but as one-star is the minimum rating, this can underreport the gap between a one-star and a two-star review.

Finally, an ordinal variable can be numeric in some scenarios.[19] Continuing with the example above, Amazon product ratings can be analyzed as both numeric and categorical variables. For instance, we can calculate the mean rating of a product numerically (i.e. 3.5 stars) and also split ratings into categories,

---

[19] Martha K. Smith, "Common Mistakes in Using Statistics," *University of Texas at Austin - Department of Mathematics*, viewed March 12 2019, https://web.ma.utexas.edu/users/mks/statmistakes/ordinal.html

such as separating all five-star reviews to analyze "true fans." The flexibility of ordinal variables will depend on what is being measured and whether it can be aggregated.

Boolean

Boolean variables are binary values that produce one of two set outcomes, such as yes/no and true/false. Like categorical variables, they can be presented in integer form but strictly as "0" (False) and "1" (True). Boolean and categorical variables can also overlap, i.e. Female (0) and Male (1).

Continuous vs Discrete

Aside from set variable types (including numeric, categorical, TimeDate, and Boolean), variables can also be characterized as *discrete* or *continuous*.

Discrete variables are variables of a finite value and cannot be aggregated or mathematically manipulated with other variable observations. Examples include suburb of residence and payment method for a transaction (as there is generally only one acceptable value). Even categorical variables described in numbers, such as zip codes and customer ID numbers, meet the criteria of discrete as they cannot be aggregated like natural numbers. As a general rule of thumb, categorical, TimeDate, and Boolean variables are discrete in value.

Continuous variables, conversely, are infinite and compatible with mathematical operations such as addition, subtraction, division, etc. Numeric variables, including integers and floating-point numbers, are therefore considered continuous as they can be aggregated or manipulated as natural numbers. Continuous numbers, though, tend to be expressed as floating-point numbers, whereas integer numbers are often used as symbols for discrete categorical variables and Boolean variables (0 and 1). Thus, judging whether an integer is continuous or discrete involves special consideration of what that value actually means, i.e. 4000 for monthly salary (continuous) and 4 for the number of animal legs (discrete).

Example Variables	Variable Type	Continuous	Discrete
Annual salary of employees	Numeric	✓	
Income bracket	Numeric: Interval	✓	✓
Gender income comparison	Numeric: Ratio	✓	
Film genre	Categorical		✓
5-star review system	Categorical: Ordinal	✓	✓
User timestamps	TimeDate		✓
Married (True/False)	Boolean		✓

Table 6: Examples of discrete and continuous variables. Interval and ordinal variables can be considered both discrete and continuous depending on their context.

Recognizing whether a variable is discrete or continuous is important when analyzing your data, as the quality of the variable (discrete, continuous, or both) will determine its compatibility with the selected algorithm. Certain algorithms that quantify relationships between variables only accept continuous variables, whereas other algorithms such as gradient boosting can take in both discrete and continuous variables as part of a single prediction model.

Lastly, keep in mind that variables also wear multiple hats. One variable can be simultaneously described as continuous, numeric, interval, and independent (i.e. **$50,000** in salary) and another as discrete, nominal, ordinal, and dependent (**Senior Manager**). Recognizing each hat leaves clues as to whether the variable can be inspected quantitatively as well as which algorithms are compatible.

## 4

DATA SCRUBBING

While the following techniques seldom grab students' attention like the chords of individual algorithms, data scrubbing methods are the unheralded accompanists of any good data analytics production. The goal of data scrubbing is to clean the dataset in preparation for machine processing. This ensures that what's fed to the algorithm is compatible and relevant for analysis.

For data practitioners, the data scrubbing process generally claims most of their time and effort. Dumping an unaltered dataset into a complex algorithmic model rarely works, as seldom can the data be analyzed in the form it was collected. Missing values, duplicate information, redundant variables, and potential data collection errors can easily conspire to derail the model's capacity to dispense valuable insight. The nearest neighbors algorithm, which computes the spatial distance between data points, returns an immediate error message with the presence of one missing value.

Data scrubbing also extends beyond amending sub-par data. Unnecessarily large datasets, for example, amplify the processing time and threshold of computational resources required for data analysis, and in some cases, the algorithm won't run to completion within a reasonable period of time. The fact that each algorithm imposes requirements on the composition of input data can also lead to an impasse. Some algorithms only accept numeric values and not, for example, strings of letters used to describe categories, i.e. "Indie Rock," "Pop," and "Classical Music."

Preparing your data in accordance with your chosen algorithm helps to ensure accuracy and the smooth running of your model. Specific techniques include filling missing values, removing irrelevant columns (features), synthesizing rows (items) into components, and converting non-numeric categories into integers. These methods help to separate the signal from the noise, lower the threshold of computational resources required for processing, and reduce total processing time.

We'll now delve into specific methods and accompanying examples of the main data scrubbing techniques.

Variable Selection

Contrary to popular opinion, more data is not always a precursor to a deeper level of insight and understanding. This is the counter-argument made by Bruce Schneier in *Data and Goliath: The Hidden Battles to Collect Your Data and Control Your World.*

"When looking for the needle, the last thing you want to do is pile lots more hay on it,"[20] writes Schneier in response to how adding irrelevant data (about innocent people) is counter-productive for spotting a potential terrorist attack.

Data isn't equal, and some variables are more valuable than others—especially when there's an overlap in information across two or more variables. Similar to stocking a vending machine for commercial gain, utmost care should be taken with what data you pack into your model. Business owners don't stock their vending machines to the brim with anything they can find. Likewise, variable selection relies on tailoring supply to dispense what's valuable and relevant.

To understand the decision path behind variable selection, let's take a look at a sample dataset. This is an excerpt from a larger

---

[20] Bruce Schneier, "Data and Goliath: The Hidden Battles to Collect Your Data and Control Your World," *W. W. Norton & Company*, First Edition, 2016.

dataset documenting crowdfunding campaigns on the website Kickstarter.com.

ID	Name	Category	Currency	Goal	Launched	Pledged	State
100000 2330	The Songs of Adelaide & Abullah	Poetry	GBP	1000	2015-08-11 12:12:28	0	Failed
100000 4038	Where is Hank?	Narrative Film	USD	45000	2013-09-09 00:20:50	220	Failed
100000 7540	ToshiCapital Rekordz Needs Help to Complete Album	Music	USD	5000	2012-03-17 03:24:11	1	Failed
100001 1046	Community Film Project: The Art of Neighborhood Filmmaking	Film & Video	USD	19500	2015-07-04 08:35:03	1283	Canceled
100001 4025	Monarch Espresso Bar	Restaurants	USD	50000	2016-02-26 13:38:27	52375	Successful
100002 3410	Support Solar Roasted Coffee & Green Energy! SolarCoffee.co	Food	USD	1000	2014-12-01 18:30:44	1205	Successful
100003 0581	Chaser Strips. Our Strips make Shots their B*tch!	Drinks	USD	25000	2016-02-01 20:05:12	453	Failed
100003 4518	SPIN - Premium Retractable In-Ear Headphones with Mic	Product Design	USD	125000	2014-04-24 18:14:43	8233	Canceled
100004 195	STUDIO IN THE SKY - A Documentary Feature Film	Documentary	USD	65000	2014-07-11 21:55:48	6240.57	Canceled
100004 721	Of Jesus and Madmen	Nonfiction	CAD	2500	2013-09-09 18:19:37	0	Failed

Table 7: Sample dataset of Kickstarter campaigns

We can see that the dataset has eight variables, and the campaigns range from film projects to music to products, poetry, and other categories of creative projects. Each funding campaign seeks support from the Kickstarter community in the form of financial pledges. As can be ascertained from the sample dataset, not all campaigns receive funding, and many campaigns are canceled or fail to reach their fundraising goal.

Although this dataset doesn't have many variables, certain clustering analysis techniques work more reliably with fewer variables. Clustering algorithms conclude how data points interrelate by measuring the distance between each data point, which can lead to extended computations as more variables are added. Also, if we limit the analysis to two or three variables, the results can be mapped on a 2-D or 3-D scatterplot. Conversely, persisting with eight variables eliminates the option of visualizing the results (humans can visualize up to four dimensions but two or three is preferable) and maximizes processing time. For a simple algorithm like nearest neighbors clustering analysis (discussed in Chapter 9)[21] two or three variables are generally recommended.

The choice of variables, though, depends on the goals of your analysis and what algorithm you choose to employ. While interesting patterns might exist regarding the **Name** of a given campaign, natural language processing techniques might not be a priority and other variables are more relevant to your analysis.

On initial inspection, we might also consider dropping the **ID** variable. As each ID number acts as a unique identifier, this variable may not generate significant insight other than to reinforce the fact that each campaign is unique. However, it's still possible for patterns to emerge when the ID variable is cross-analyzed with a second variable such as the **Pledged** variable. Campaigns with a low ID number (i.e. below 1000025000) may attract a higher volume of pledges as these campaigns were funded prior to an oversupply of campaigns on the platform. The decision to include the ID variable would require domain knowledge specific to the condition of the number and to confirm whether ID numbers are assigned chronologically, such that lower numbers are assigned to older campaigns and higher numbers to more recent campaigns.

In other cases, variable selection is relatively straightforward. Some datasets, for example, include both the name of a user's country and their country code in separate columns, i.e. ZA for South Africa and UK for the United Kingdom. In such cases, there's little harm in removing one of these two variables (country and country code) as they contain the same information.

---

[21] The nearest neighbors technique forms clusters by merging data points with one or more nearby data points. Discussed further in Chapter 9.

Lastly, it's common for data scientists to fiddle with variable selection and observe the results, as well as revisit their choice of variables later in the model's development.

Merging Variables

Similar to the goal of choosing variables, merging variables attempts to limit the number of variables fed to the model based on relevancy. However, rather than exclude variables, merging combines related variables in a way that attempts to preserve maximum information. Merging variables helps to reduce the total number of variables and preserves more information than outright removing them. The prime benefit of merging variables, though, comes with lowering the number of dimensions, which makes it easier to visualize relationships between variables.

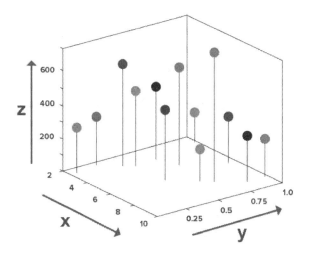

Figure 5: A three-dimensional scatterplot with variables represented on the x, y, and z axes respectively.

While machines are able to work competently with high-dimensional data, the maximum number of variables we can plot on a scatterplot is four, with the fourth dimension being time. In general, it's easier to visualize data using two or three dimensions, but a 4-D visual representation can be useful for doctors who want to visualize a patient's internal anatomy moving in real-time, for example.[22]

The benefit of merging variables is that we can take high-dimensional data with four or five variables and transform it into a lower dimension using two or three variables. This makes it possible to visualize the data and spot patterns and regularities, especially when zooming out of the data on a graphical interface. Conversely, analyzing too many dimensions (more than four) makes it impossible to visualize patterns in the data.

Variables, though, must be closely related in order for them to be compressed. We can't merge two unrelated variables; there must be some degree of overlap or relationship between variables to create a new variable. "Room length" and "room width," for example, can be multiplied, merged, and relabeled as "room area." Returning to our Kickstarter dataset, we can reduce the number of dimensions by combining the **Currency** variable with the **Goal** and **Pledged** variables respectively. This works by standardizing the **Goal** and **Pledged** variables into one currency, I.E. USD, and then removing the original **Currency** variable from the dataset. In this way, three variables become two. The original **Goal** and **Pledged** columns therefore need to be updated using the relevant exchange rate.

As highlighted in Table 8, only a small number of changes are needed. The two campaigns expressed in GBP and CAD did not receive any **Pledged** money and therefore remain at 0. Their **Goal** values, meanwhile, are multiplied by *1.32 for GDP and *0.74 for CAD respectively.

The Songs of Adelaide & Abullah
£1000 → 1000 * 1.32 = 1320 (USD)

---

22 Plotting four dimensions is beyond the limits of the book format.

Of Jesus and Madmen

$2500 CAD → 2500 * 0.74 = 1850 (USD)

ID	Name	Currency	Goal_USD	Pledged	State
100000 2330	The Songs of Adelaide & Abullah	GBP	1320	0	Failed
100000 4038	Where is Hank?	USD	45000	220	Failed
100000 7540	ToshiCapital Rekordz Needs Help to Complete Album	USD	5000	1	Failed
100001 1046	Community Film Project: The Art of Neighborhood Filmmaking	USD	19500	1283	Canceled
100001 4025	Monarch Espresso Bar	USD	50000	52375	Successful
100002 3410	Support Solar Roasted Coffee & Green Energy! SolarCoffee.co	USD	1000	1205	Successful
100003 0581	Chaser Strips. Our Strips make Shots their B*tch!	USD	25000	453	Failed
100003 4518	SPIN - Premium Retractable In-Ear Headphones with Mic	USD	125000	8233	Canceled
100004 195	STUDIO IN THE SKY - A Documentary Feature Film	USD	65000	6240.57	Canceled
100004 721	Of Jesus and Madmen	CAD	1850	0	Failed

Table 8: Updates are highlighted and marked in bold case

There could, though, be a downside to this update if the currency of the campaign affects the outcome. For instance, the two campaigns that didn't receive funding were both advertised in a currency other than US dollars. Variable selection is not always a clear pathway, and the onus is on us, as the model architect, to ask the right questions about our data.

One-hot Encoding

Formatting is an important consideration in data analytics and sometimes you need to transform variables into a different format for the algorithm to run. The **State** (Failed, Canceled,

Successful) feature of a Kickstarter campaign, for example, can't be processed by a clustering or regression algorithm in its original format because the values are expressed as a string (text). To fix this problem, we can transform the **State** variable values into integer form while preserving them as categorical and discrete using a technique called one-hot encoding.

ID	Name	Goal	Pledged	State
1000002330	The Songs of Adelaide & Abullah	1000	0	0
1000004038	Where is Hank?	45000	220	0
1000007540	ToshiCapital Rekordz Needs Help to Complete Album	5000	1	0
1000011046	Community Film Project: The Art of Neighborhood Filmmaking	19500	1283	0
1000014025	Monarch Espresso Bar	50000	52375	1
1000023410	Support Solar Roasted Coffee & Green Energy! SolarCoffee.co	1000	1205	1
1000030581	Chaser Strips. Our Strips make Shots their B*tch!	25000	453	0
1000034518	SPIN - Premium Retractable In-Ear Headphones with Mic	125000	8233	0
1000041 95	STUDIO IN THE SKY - A Documentary Feature Film	65000	6240.57	0
1000047 21	Of Jesus and Madmen	2500	0	0

Table 9: Example of one-hot encoding applied to the column on the far right

This technique transforms discrete variables into a binary format, represented as "1" or "0"—"True" or "False." In the case of our Kickstarter campaign, we can assign 0 to both Canceled and Failed campaigns and assign 1 to Successful campaigns as shown in Table 9.

This makes it possible to input the variable into a model and analyze its mathematical relationship with other variables.

Binning

Using a technique called *binning,* we can convert similar numeric or timestamp values into a category using a discrete integer. Be careful to note that binning is different from one-hot encoding, where we converted categories into a Boolean value of "0" or "1".

Binning is useful in cases where the gap between numeric or timestamp information is arbitrary or overly specific (information creep). In the case of the Kickstarter campaign dataset, there's information creep with hours, minutes, and seconds included in the timestamp. Due to a minor separation between campaigns, the specificity of the timestamp is bound to treat each campaign as unique. Grouping campaigns that are similar to each other based on a less specific timestamp, such as month and year, might make it easier to spot patterns and find groups of related data points.

Using binning, we can subsequently remove day, hour, minutes, and seconds from the **Launched** variable and convert it to a categorical identifier (expressed as an integer) based on year and month.

ID	Name	Goal	Launched	Pledged	State
1000002 330	The Songs of Adelaide & Abullah	1000	1	0	0
1000004 038	Where is Hank?	45000	2	220	0
1000007 540	ToshiCapital Rekordz Needs Help to Complete Album	5000	3	1	0
1000011 046	Community Film Project: The Art of Neighborhood Filmmaking	19500	4	1283	0
1000014 025	Monarch Espresso Bar	50000	5	52375	1
1000023 410	Support Solar Roasted Coffee & Green Energy! SolarCoffee.co	1000	6	1205	1
1000030 581	Chaser Strips. Our Strips make Shots their B*tch!	25000	5	453	0
1000034 518	SPIN - Premium Retractable In-Ear Headphones with Mic	125000	7	8233	0
1000041 95	STUDIO IN THE SKY - A Documentary Feature Film	65000	8	6240.57	0
1000047 21	Of Jesus and Madmen	2500	2	0	0

Table 10: Changes to Launched variable highlighted using binning

2015-08-11 12:12:28 ➔ 2015-08 = 1

2013-09-09 00:20:50 ➔ 2013-09 = **2**

2012-03-17 03:24:11 ➔ 2012-03 = 3

2015-07-04 08:35:03 ➔ 2015-07 = 4

2016-02-26 13:38:27 ➔ 2016-02 = **5**

2014-12-01 18:30:44 ➔ 2014-12 = 6

2016-02-01 20:05:12 ➔ 2016-02 = **5**

2014-04-24 18:14:43 ➔ 2014-04 = 7

2014-07-11 21:55:48 ➔ 2014-07 = 8

2013-09-09 18:19:37 ➜ 2013-09 = **2**

The campaigns "Monarch Espresso Bar" and "Chaser Strips" are now assigned to the same bin, labeled as "5," as they were both launched in February 2016, and "Where is Hank" and "Of Jesus and Madmen" are labeled as "2." Depending on your goals and dataset, you could opt to bin timestamps according to the year or by another variant. Binning timestamps into an integer value also makes it easier to plot and cross-analyze against other variables.

Lastly, binning can be used to convert variables into a Boolean value (True/False, 0 or 1) or a category string (i.e. small, medium, large).

Data Retention

It's important not to misconstrue data scrubbing with the permanent removal and manipulation of data. Each of the data scrubbing techniques explored in this chapter should be isolated from the source data in a code notebook or a graphical interface such as Tableau, separate from the source file.

It's vital to maintain the integrity of the source data as you may wish to revisit variables that were previously removed or manipulated. As a data scientist, it's difficult to predict what you or your colleagues might ask of the data in the future. Model design is, after all, an iterative process. To this end, it's usually safer to hold the data under a data retention policy. For some industries, this may even be a legal requirement. Hospitals, for example, must retain petabytes of patient records for multiple decades to comply with local regulatory requirements.

In regards to the monetary cost of retaining data, it's also becoming cheaper to store and archive huge volumes of data using long-term storage solutions such as Amazon Glacier that allow you to archive data for as little as $0.004 a month per gigabyte of data.

## 5

METHODOLOGY

There are innumerable ways of extracting value from data and choosing an appropriate method demands special consideration. This includes considering the composition of your input data, the computational resources available at your disposal, and finding an algorithm that matches your output goal. The algorithm, however, sits behind another organizing system or methodology. Examples of these overarching systems include machine learning, data mining, and descriptive analytics, which control the scope, design, and quality of the model.

Although certain algorithms including linear regression and clustering analysis are used across disciplines, they are applied differently depending on the methodology chosen. Data mining models, for example, formulate predictions based exclusively on input data, whereas machine learning can be used to compare known combinations of input and output data to build a model for predicting the output of new input data. Descriptive analytics incorporates a different methodology that summarizes data rather than deriving predictions based on inference.

To understand the differences between data mining, machine learning, and descriptive analytics, we first need to look at the role of statistics, which provides the foundation for various methodologies.

Statistics

If we think of data mining, machine learning, and descriptive analytics as the downstream branches of data analytics, then statistics is the upstream source of all three methods.

Statistics involves studying how data is collected, organized, analyzed, interpreted, and presented with the primary goal of determining the meaning of the data and whether variations, if any, are meaningful or due merely to chance. The field of statistics also splits into two distinct subfields called *descriptive statistics* and *inferential statistics*.

Descriptive statistics encompasses methods for describing data, such as variance (how the data varies), central tendency (the middle of the dataset), ratios between variables, and range (minimum and maximum values). These methods help to summarize known and meaningful trends in order to provide a clearer picture of the data.

The second branch of statistical analysis is predicated on inference, which is an exploratory method that involves characterizing or forming predictions about a population using an information sample drawn from that population. This method relies on forming predictions based on probability and goes beyond summarizing known patterns in the data. A large majority of statistical analysis is based on inferential statistics and many sophisticated techniques have been devised and developed to facilitate this type of analysis.[23]

In sum, inferential statistical analysis is adept at making predictions, whereas descriptive statistics is convenient for summarizing information. The choice between these two methods depends on what you want to find and what data is available. *Is the purpose of analysis to directly describe the data collected or to generalize a larger dataset you can't study directly?*

Descriptive statistical analysis, for example, is useful when all relevant information is available and analysis is contained to one

---

[23] Sarah Boslaugh, "Statistics in a Nutshell," *O'Reilly Media*, Second Edition, 2012.

dataset. Inferential statistics, meanwhile, applies to cases where existing information is limited or for making predictions about events occurring outside the dataset. Comprehensive datasets about future events, for instance, don't reliably exist, and one might need to look at a historical dataset to project predictions regarding future events. Equally, when looking at the past, gaps in record-keeping might inhibit descriptive analysis and necessitate an inferential approach, such as analyzing daily life in ancient societies. In either case, the best we can do is analyze the data that does exist and generate inferences that extend to what we are attempting to predict. By analyzing clay tablets from ancient Mesopotamia we can infer details regarding daily life without a comprehensive dataset from that period.

Given that we're trying to estimate something that can't be measured directly and input data isn't truly representative of the event we're predicting, there is the possibility of sampling errors, missing values, variance, or random chance negatively affecting the results. The only reliable way of proving the results as 100% accurate is to analyze the full target dataset, but that would render the analysis descriptive rather than inference-based. A natural goal of inferential statistics, therefore, is to minimize error and to utilize probability as a tool to predict the most likely outcome.

Understanding the distinction between inferential and descriptive analysis will help you decide which methodology to take with your own data analytics project. If you plan to interpret the past and your data is detailed in nature, descriptive analytics is a fast and accurate methodology to implement and explain patterns. Conversely, if your job is to predict future events or interpret what has happened in the past based on limited information, inferential methods such as data mining and machine learning enable you to integrate probabilistic methods to make predictions that extend beyond the data.

Lastly, it's common practice to start data analysis using descriptive statistics to gain a general sense of the dataset, including range, standard deviation, variable correlation, and central tendency measures (i.e. mean and median), before switching to inferential methods. In data analytics, you can never be too familiar with your data.

Descriptive Analytics

Descriptive analytics is the less subjective side of data analytics and is a common tool in our everyday work lives. The more in-vogue term for descriptive methods is "analytics," which is the handle name of many well-known tools offered by Google, Twitter, Pinterest, YouTube, and JetPack.

From sales numbers to LinkedIn profile views, analytics helps us compress complex information into a convenient and easily readable format. One of the popular examples of descriptive analytics is the web analytics service Google Analytics. Using this online software, users can chart the inflow and outflow of web traffic to their website and view clear metrics that summarize user behavior, including the ratio of page clicks to page views, the volume of daily visitors, and the annual number of returning visitors. These metrics provide a convenient and concise summary of historical data generated from a potentially vast number of stand-alone events.

Another use case of descriptive methods is sports analysis, in which player and team metrics are recorded, tabulated, and summarized. As with web traffic, individual events are meticulously logged and recorded, making it viable to derive insight with a high degree of accuracy (beyond basic collection or interpretation errors).

To sketch an accurate portrait of the data, descriptive analytics favors instances where the data is well-documented and standardized into a single pool of information. Big data, for instance, is difficult to synthesize using descriptive methods because taking data from a variety of sources and formats is difficult to standardize, summarize, and process. The size of the data may also necessitate the need to extract representative samples and use that data to draw conclusions about the dataset, which necessitates an inferential approach.

A commercial example of descriptive analytics is Juwai.com, an Australian-founded online real estate platform, which lists overseas properties to its user base of Chinese investors. Based on real-time data collected from users' search activity on their site, Juwai is able to collect data 6-12 months ahead of the real estate purchasing cycle and earlier than most other parties. This data is then summarized for trends, packaged as insight, and sold to hedge fund managers and investment bankers. One of the dominant trends when I met with Juwai in Beijing in 2016 was user interest in Japanese real estate. A historically low Yen and growing exposure to Japan via outbound tourism had led to strong demand, which was driving Chinese-language search queries for Japanese properties in urban hotspots and in proximity to universities.

Lastly, it's worth noting that as data collection becomes increasingly automated and secondary in nature, descriptive analytics alone may not be enough to gain an advantage in a competitive business environment. With business managers doubling requests for predictions and alternative data rather than summaries of existing data, interest is shifting towards inferential methods and discovering unknown patterns in complex datasets. It is possible, though, to integrate descriptive analytics into the preliminary stage of data analysis to prepare the dataset for further investigation using inferential methods such as data mining and machine learning.

Inferential Methods

While history has a quirky habit of repeating itself, it's anything but precise. Elite athletes embark on extended winning streaks but seldom do they repeat their feats with split-second consistency. Similarly, economic downturns replicate or exceed financial losses of the past but they arise from new fault lines and reverberate over the market with changing levels of despair.

Predicting the future requires a certain degree of "guesswork" and one way of accounting for natural variance is *split validation*. This technique involves isolating and analyzing a portion of the data and then testing the results against the other subset of the data. The first segment is called the training data, which typically represents 70% to 80% of the original data. The training data is used by the machine to identify patterns and form a model to make predictions. The remaining 20% to 30% of data is called the test data and is used as a new input to evaluate and validate the accuracy of the model developed from the training data. The results from the test data can then be used to assess prediction accuracy.

As the training and test data are split randomly, they are likely to contain some level of variance, thereby mimicking the presence of random phenomena found in real-life events. This helps to build a generalized model with a buffer zone that can absorb variance rather than remaining highly tuned to one set of data, a common problem known as *overfitting*.[24]

As a key tenet of machine learning and data mining, split validation also enables data scientists to extract patterns from very large datasets. By extracting a training set and deliberately restricting the intake of data, they can make general assumptions regarding large amounts of data that would be difficult and time-consuming to deliver using descriptive methods. Data scientists, for instance, can analyze a random sample of Spotify users to infer user preferences rather than analyze the listening behavior of every user on the platform.

A key principle of inferential statistics is that the prediction can never be 100% certain. This is because the sample data isn't 100% representative of the full population due to some margin of error and the presence of random phenomena.

---

[24] There is also an inverse concept called *underfitting*, which occurs when the model is overly simple and hasn't scratched the surface of underlying patterns in the data. Underfitting can lead to inaccurate predictions by the model using both the training data and test data as input.

Machine learning and data mining are based on inference because the model is designed according to the training data, which in itself is sample data. Although the model processes both the training and test sets (at separate intervals), it's from the training data alone that the model is built. The test data is never decoded and should not be used to create the prediction model. It is only used to make predictions based on rules extracted from the training data. The model is therefore inferential because the training (70%) and test (30%) sets are assessed individually (and not collectively) to infer predictions about the full dataset. In addition, you can't train the model with both portions of the data and aggregate the results in order to perfectly understand the full dataset. Random variation at the time of the dataset's split will lead to unique patterns in the training and test sets that aren't representative of the dataset prior to the split.

Lastly, inferential methods can complement scenarios where data is unavailable. Spotify, for example, can't access a full dataset containing songs users have listened to on other mediums, such as radio, music concerts, and old iPod playlists. Thus, rather than implement descriptive methods to summarize known user preferences and limit what songs it recommends, Spotify observes the behavior of other users with similar characteristics to infer the music tastes of each target user.

A practical demonstration of both inferential and descriptive analysis using Python can be found in the supplementary chapters found at the end of this book.

Data Mining

As an interdisciplinary approach, data mining can be defined in several ways. Jiawei Han, Micheline Kamber, and Jian Pei in *Data Mining: Concepts and Techniques* define data mining as "the convenient extraction of patterns representing knowledge implicitly stored or captured in large databases, data warehouses, the Web, other massive information repositories, or data streams."[25] Data mining is also referred to as *knowledge discovery from data* or by the abbreviation *KDD*. Prior to industry convergence on data mining and KDD in the 1990s, identical or similar methods were previously referred to as *database mining*, *information retrieval*, and other names.

The evolution of data mining/KDD techniques followed the development of information technology in the early 1980s and an urgent need to make sense of patterns from large and complicated datasets.[26] Data mining subsequently became the dominant path for interpreting large and complex datasets, and mining the vast reserves of data stored in data warehouses.

What originally made data mining distinct from other categories of data processing was its unique focus on discovery and exploration. Unlike standard statistical models, which set out to quantify a defined hypothesis (prediction) as "likely" or "unlikely," data mining has no starting point in the form of a hypothesis. Similar to randomly drilling a hole into the earth's crust, data mining isn't committed to a set hypothesis of what it will dig up. Instead, it seeks to find new and unmined patterns and relationships that aren't immediately apparent. Data mining also relies on domain expertise from human operators regarding which variables and patterns to probe (or to avoid). This is contrary to machine learning, which utilizes ongoing exposure to data as a mechanism for feedback, a process better known as *self-learning*.

Data mining is well-established in the industry, and there are many examples we can look at to understand its benefits. One interesting example is the backstory behind Netflix's investment in the TV series *House of Cards*. Before purchasing the broadcasting rights for the popular American TV series, Netflix

---

[25] Jiawei Han, Micheline Kamber & Jian Pei, "Data Mining: Concepts and Techniques (The Morgan Kaufmann Series in Data Management Systems)," *Morgan Kauffmann,* 3rd Edition, 2011.
[26] Jiawei Han, Micheline Kamber & Jian Pei, "Data Mining: Concepts and Techniques (The Morgan Kaufmann Series in Data Management Systems)," *Morgan Kauffmann,* 3rd Edition, 2011.

conducted analysis based on the correlation they extracted from mining their user data. Specifically, Netflix identified that:

- Netflix users who watched the film *The Social Network,* directed by David Fincher, typically viewed it from beginning to end.
- The British version of *House of Cards* was well-watched.
- Those who watched the British version of *House of Cards* also enjoyed watching films featuring Kevin Spacey, and/or films directed by David Fincher.

These synergies, based on correlation, ultimately informed Netflix's decision to purchase the broadcasting rights to the U.S. web television series. Prior to data mining, there was little way of finding or knowing about this relationship because there was no predefined category in their database to label this relationship.

Selecting an appropriate problem for data mining is another important factor. Given the time and financial cost of mining large amounts of data, it's important to identify problems worth solving, especially when there's no guarantee of generating useful insight. Consideration of your business targets and (service or customer) gaps in the market are useful places to start when conducting data mining analysis.

Machine Learning

As a hot example of inferential analysis, machine learning gives computers the ability to learn without being explicitly programmed. While the theory of machine learning has existed since the late 1950s, only recently has it eclipsed data mining in popularity and widespread adoption. Self-learning, the key tenet of machine learning, is a complex process and the availability of data as well as the cost of data processing were for a long time inhibitors to its development. Now, machine learning is a cornerstone of contemporary innovation, alongside blockchain technology and the Internet of Things. Its application spans finding matches on dating apps to detecting bank fraud and assisting marketers to predict which users will click 'buy'.

While inferential modeling and split validation are key elements of machine learning (akin to data mining), they don't explain the ability of machines to learn without direct programming. This question leads us to the study of supervised learning, unsupervised learning, and reinforcement learning, which reveal the mechanics of self-learning based on three distinct ways of analyzing input and output variables.

Supervised Learning

The goal of supervised learning is to uncover patterns that connect inputs with their output and apply those rules to predict future instances from new input data. Through the observation of existing data, the model knows what inputs (independent variables) produce a given output (dependent variable).

In the case of language analysis, for example, the machine is fed thousands of audio examples of different dialects. Each dialect is pre-classified or tagged as a specific dialect, i.e. Cockney, Irish, New York, Australian, and Welsh. The name of the dialect provides the output (or target) value. The model then analyzes the input values for each output value, including analyzing pitch, sentence composition, word selection, and sentence length for each input-output example. Over time, the model finds patterns and rules to write a model that predicts a dialect (output) based exclusively on its input variables.

Predictions are generally accurate, but supervised learning unravels when the map doesn't correspond to the territory. This problem occurs when the model is fed new data containing different patterns from what was observed in the training data.

Unsupervised Learning

Unlike supervised learning where the model is presented with pre-labeled input and output combinations, unsupervised learning is "unsupervised," meaning there are no known outputs to act as reference points. Instead, the goal of unsupervised learning is to analyze input values to find patterns and create new outputs—similar to data mining.

A common way of deciphering patterns among input data is to split that data into groups using clustering analysis. Imagine that we feed the model text excerpts translated into various languages, including Mandarin Chinese, Japanese, Korean, Italian, Turkish, Dutch, Georgian, and Spanish. Each of these languages is described by input variables including the number of worldwide speakers, category of writing system (i.e. Cyrillic, Chinese characters, Latin alphabet), longitude range of native-speaking countries, and language family.

Using clustering analysis, the three Asian languages will likely cluster as a group based on longitude, writing system, and language family, which can be explained by regular visits from Korean and Japanese scholars to Tang dynasty China starting in the 7th Century AD. This cluster of languages won't be explicitly labeled by the unsupervised learning algorithm as "East Asian languages." The cluster is formed according to shared attributes and not from the machine's explicit knowledge of an existing category/output such as "East Asian languages."

Finding unconsidered clusters of data points is an exciting part of unsupervised learning. For instance, without unsupervised learning, you might not have been aware of the similarities in sentence structure and word order between Korean, Japanese, and Turkish, which don't fall under an obvious banner of language classification.[27] This might be useful information for Turkish speakers considering the acquisition of a second language. Unsupervised learning also helps to generate new categories, such as the formation of all languages spoken by

---

[27] This analogy is an example only. A proposed term "Altaic" has been largely rejected by linguist experts as a family of languages that would include central Eurasian and Siberian languages as well as Korean and Japanese.

more than 50 million people or languages spoken between the tropic of Capricorn and the Arctic circle.

Reinforcement Learning

The third and final category of machine learning is reinforcement learning, which is the most advanced and exciting example of machine intelligence. The goal of reinforcement learning is to achieve a specific output or sequence of outputs by randomly trialing a large number of possible input combinations and grading their performance.

This desired goal or output could be to win a game of chess or operate a robotic arm and assemble a specified widget. Through random trial and error as well as a process of elimination, the machine attempts various combinations and measures the distance from the desired output. In the case of chess, this might mean reducing moves that lead to losing while emphasizing moves that lead to winning.

This type of machine learning is computationally demanding as the absence of input data requires the machine to generate its own random input data and compare the outcome of its results with the target output. It also takes a massive number of attempts to achieve its intended goal. The upside of reinforcement learning is that it helps to create previously unseen combinations of data inputs that can't be found using supervised or unsupervised learning.

Playing the strategy board game Go, a reinforcement learning program called AlphaGo discovered moves that were deemed exceptional and previously unseen by veteran commentators of the game. One move was considered so unexpected that it unraveled the world's number-one-ranked Go player, Lee So-dol, in a five-match series held in South Korea in 2016. AlphaGo went on to win four matches in the five-match series. You can watch the Netflix documentary AlphaGo to see some of the play-by-play drama unfold.

Machine Learning Vs Data Mining

To close out this chapter, let's review how machine learning diverges from its close cousin *data mining*, which both fall under the broad umbrella of data science.

Within data science, there is a special grouping of disciplines in artificial intelligence that includes machine learning. Data mining isn't considered artificial intelligence because it relies on human input and feedback and therefore belongs to its own separate discipline within data science. There is, however, a substantial spillover between machine learning and data mining, and the two terms are sometimes used interchangeably by non-experts and even database specialists. This is because some data mining techniques apply the same algorithms applied in machine learning, such as *k*-means clustering and regression analysis.

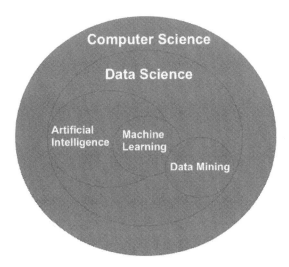

Figure 6: Interrelationships between various data-related fields

While data mining and machine learning draw from many of the same algorithms and make predictions based on inference, machine learning operates a layer removed from human interference and enjoys a broader scope of utility. Data mining, meanwhile, focuses exclusively on input data to generate an output and excels at finding unknown relationships.

Data mining also treats data as noise. Like scrubbing rocks and wildlife after a major oil spill, data mining removes what isn't desired before sitting back and waiting for the next major spill. Machine learning, on the other hand, learns from the data. When Google compares your first and second search query and makes an inference about the web content you're searching for, it isn't a matter of cleaning up swathes of data but rather a gradual process of learning from exposure to data. Machine learning models are therefore constantly learning and adapting to new data inputs—big and small—and storing those values to inform and optimize future predictions. It's this ability to learn from experience over time that makes machine learning an essential cog in artificial intelligence and unique from other techniques such as data mining.

Technique	Input is Known	Output is Known	Methodology
Data Mining	✓		Analyzes inputs to generate an unknown output.
Supervised Learning	✓	✓	Analyzes combinations of known inputs and outputs to predict future outputs based on new input data.
Unsupervised Learning	✓		Analyzes inputs to generate an output—algorithms may differ from data mining.
Reinforcement Learning		✓	Randomly trials a high number of input variables to produce a desired output.

Table 11: Comparison of techniques based on the utility of input and output data

## 6

ALGORITHMS

What electricity supplied and achieved during the Industrial Revolution, computer algorithms are tipped to perfect in the 21st Century. For those watching, the possibilities are both dizzying and slightly unsettling in terms of what might materialize. Rather than ponder the opportunities and perils of re-coding human existence in the 21st Century, this chapter breaks down what these algorithms are and why they're more familiar than most people think.

While it's tempting to picture algorithms as a recent phenomenon or the latest tactic to manipulate our online behavior, this sweeping synopsis fails to acknowledge that humankind has always been programmed by pre-defined formulas. The big difference is that algorithms are now embedded in silicon and network connections rather than just natural and physical bodies.

An algorithm is a sequence of steps that reacts to cues and changing patterns to generate a decision or output. When we wake up in the morning, our brain and body are wired to follow a series of well-defined steps that lead to an output (target value). For many of us, the target value is arriving at the office on time. Following natural cues such as sunlight, room temperature, and a biochemical urge for sustenance, our body reacts to these data points as we complete a series of actions that lead us to our target value. This sequence of steps might include fumbling for the snooze button, a beeline to the bathroom, a cluster of tasks under the collective banner of caffeine and carbohydrates, wardrobe decisions, a last-minute search for the house keys, and shutting the front door behind us. The sum of sunlight, room temperature, appetite, fatigue, and other natural forces vary on a daily basis, but more times than not, our internal algorithm directs us from point A to point B while reacting to many changing variables.

Using algorithmic sequencing, animals can also be programmed to respond to different variables to achieve a target output. In the early 1900s, a horse named Clever Hans became famous for performing arithmetic and other intellectual tasks. To the applause of onlookers, Clever Hans solved simple arithmetic problems by tapping his hoof on the ground to signify the correct answer to the equation. The horse seemed to have a natural aptitude for arithmetic, but a psychologist later noticed that the horse was following a simple system of steps designed to deceive his audience. Instead of finding an answer in a single lunge of equine intelligence, Clever Hans tapped his hoof until he recognized a set reaction (in the form of applause) from his trainer or the audience as a cue to stop. Clever Hans had no human problem-solving skills, or for that matter, any consciousness of arithmetic. He simply knew when to stop and how to follow orders.

Machine-based intelligence is constructed on a similar process of sequencing that falls short of human consciousness. Unlike animals and humans, machines have perfect memory and can respond to a massive intake of input data. By executing a series of steps directed by an algorithm, machines react to changing input variables to interpret patterns, make calculations, and reach decisions. This formulaic method of decision-making and reacting to variables resembles our own reasoning abilities that have been so vital in the development and evolution of our species.

As input data is constantly changing, algorithms are unique and malleable, which is true of both machine and human-based algorithms. Up until the late 19th Century, retail stores did not set a fixed price for their inventory and customers had to negotiate and process different variables to arrive at a reasonable price.[28] Relevant input variables probably included the store location, the attire of other customers, the quality of the item, and what the customer paid for a similar item in the past. As each customer referred to their own internal algorithm for evaluating a fair price based on the variables they deemed important, the final price paid by the customer differed from one person to the next.

Similarly, different algorithms are used today by Google, Yahoo, Bing, and other search engine companies in order to rank and return web pages—with no single off-the-shelf algorithm for returning search results. Each company devises its own sequence of analyzing input data based on the data it collects, the variables it deems most relevant, and the chosen weights of the algorithm, called *hyperparameters*. Also, just as Colonel Sanders' had his special algorithm for finger-licking good chicken, machine algorithms aren't always easy to replicate. Thus, while companies are unable to monopolize ownership of general algorithms such as logistic regression and gradient boosting, they can guard how they feed and implement their algorithmic models.

Over the following chapters, we'll take a look at specific techniques and the relationship between data and algorithms.

---

[28] The Quakers were responsible for the introduction of price tags because they deemed it immoral for different customers to pay different prices.

## 7

REGRESSION ANALYSIS

Regression analysis is a popular statistical technique used to model the relationship between one or more independent variables and the dependent variable. Businesses, for instance, often utilize regression to predict sales (output) based on a range of input variables including weather temperature, social media mentions, historical sales, GDP growth, and inbound tourists.

The goal of regression analysis is to find a line or curve that best describes patterns in the data. Although a single line or curve actually oversimplifies the data, it provides a useful reference point for making general predictions about future data. The quality of predictions derived from a regression line/curve is underwritten by correlation, and specifically, a coefficient of correlation, which is equal to the square root of the line's variance. A coefficient of correlation is measured between -1 and 1, with a correlation of 1 describing a perfect positive relationship and a correlation of -1 indicating a perfect negative relationship. A coefficient of 0, meanwhile, means no relationship between variables.

A negative correlation means that an increase in the independent variable leads to a subsequent decrease in the dependent variable. For example, a **house's value** (dependent variable) tends to depreciate as the **distance to the city** (independent variable) increases. Conversely, a positive correlation captures a positive relationship between variables. **House value** (dependent variable), for instance, generally appreciates in sync with **house size** (independent variable).

Linear Regression Analysis

The most basic form of regression analysis is linear regression, which generates a straight line to describe a dataset with a linear relationship between variables. The formula for linear regression is:

$$y = a + bx$$

The "y" represents the dependent variable and "x" represents the independent variable. The variable "a" represents the point where the hyperplane crosses the origin on the y-intercept and the "b" represents the hyperplane's slope and dictates the steepness of the regression line.

Let's now look at a visual demonstration of this technique.

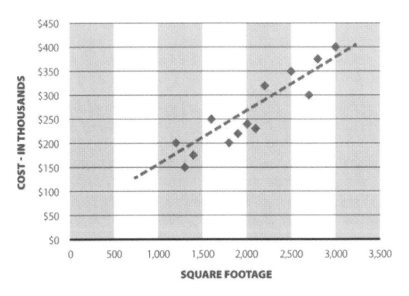

Figure 7: Example of linear regression using two variables

The two variables plotted in Figure 8 are **House Cost** and **Square Footage,** both of which represent continuous/numeric variables. **House Cost** is plotted on the vertical axis (y), and **Square Footage** is expressed along the horizontal axis (x). Each data point represents one paired measurement of both **Square Footage** and **House Cost**. As you can see, there is a total of 13 data points, denoting 13 houses from a given suburb.

As the dataset has a linear relationship, meaning that a given change in an independent variable produces a corresponding change in the dependent variable, we can plot a straight line called a hyperplane to compress the mathematical relationship between **Square Footage** and **House Cost**.

The goal of linear regression is to engineer a straight line that optimally dissects the data points so that there is a minimal distance between each data point and the hyperplane. This means that if you drew a vertical line from the hyperplane to every data point on the plot, the distance of each point would equate to the smallest possible distance of any potential hyperplane.

Another important feature of regression is *slope*. The slope can be found by referencing the hyperplane. As one variable increases, you can expect the other variable to increase by the average value denoted by the hyperplane. The slope is therefore useful for forming predictions, and these predictions become more accurate the closer the data points are to the hyperplane. If there's a significant deviation in the distance between the data points and the hyperplane, the slope is less likely to be an accurate predictor.

One of the major prerequisites of linear regression analysis is that the variables behave linearly. Plots A (positive correlation) and B (negative correlation) in Figure 8 are examples of a linear relationship, where a given change in an independent variable produces a corresponding change in the dependent variable.

In the case of plots C and D, no linear relationship exists between the two variables, making linear regression a poor option.

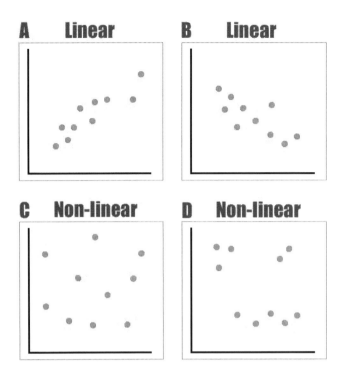

Figure 8: Examples of linear and non-linear patterns

Another potential problem is *collinearity*. This occurs when there's a strong linear correlation between two independent variables, which limits the regression model's capacity to predict the dependent variable. An example of *collinearity* would be using **liters of fuel consumed** and **liters of fuel remaining in the tank** as independent variables to predict car mileage. The two independent variables, in this case, are negatively correlated and virtually cancel each out when included in the same model. Rather, it would be better to include one variable and sideline the other variable. Height and weight are another popular example of two variables that are often highly correlated and can lead to problems with collinearity in the model.

Non-linear Regression

Non-linear regression is similar to linear regression in that it quantifies the relationship between the independent variable(s) and a dependent variable, and attempts to find an optimal line that best intersects all data points.

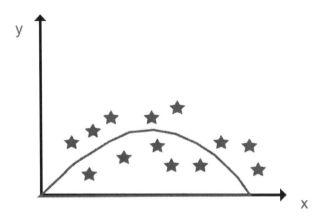

Figure 9: Example of a non-linear regression curve

A major distinction between linear regression and non-linear regression is the profile of the regression line. In linear regression, the line is perfectly straight, but in non-linear regression, the regression line is a curve or squiggle that bends to fit patterns in the data.

The other central distinction of non-linear regression is that the dependency between the independent and dependent variables is non-linear. This means that a change in an independent variable doesn't necessarily correspond to a consistent change in the value of the dependent variable. Thus, unlike linear regression, there is often no general closed-form mathematical expression for finding an optimal fit. Non-linear models are instead created through a series of approximations (iterations), typically based on a system of trial-and-error, with the Gauss-Newton method and the Levenberg-Marquardt method serving as popular techniques.

Note also that because non-linear regression has more flexibility to fit non-linear datasets, it can be prone to overfitting the training data when used in machine learning.

Exponential Regression

Another type of non-linear data is exponential data, where certain values are multiples of previous values. Examples of exponential data include population growth (think rabbits), microchip transistors (Moore's Law), investment growth, and most recently, cryptocurrency. These types of trends tend to start relatively flat but multiply rapidly with new data points.

For generalizing exponential data, a linear hyperplane is too high in the middle of the plot and too low on the far right to make reliable predictions. However, for such data, it is possible to adapt the linear regression formula as presented below:

$$y = e^{a + bx}$$

The formula has been modified so that e (the exponential constant, equal to approx. 2.71828) is now the base of what's called a natural logarithm. This produces the following curve:

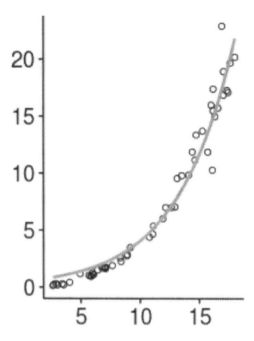

Figure 10: Exponential regression

Keep in mind also that the y variable must be a positive value (greater than zero) for this formula to work. This is due to the mathematical characteristic of e, which can only produce a positive y value as part of this formula. Alternatively, you can change any negative y values in the dataset to a small positive value or even remove those values entirely from the dataset—granted that an exponential regression curve fits with most of the remaining data points.

Strengths

+ Regression models are easy to interpret as patterns in the data are usually defined by an algebraic equation and regression line/curve.

+ Regression models are generally fast to build and run.

Weaknesses

- Regression analysis can be a weak predictor in the case of poor-quality data. Missing values, outliers, and erratic variance may conspire to derail the model's capacity to adequately analyze the data.

- Too many input variables may overcomplicate the model as each variable is integrated into the prediction equation and this may affect accuracy. The problem is pronounced when variables are non-linear or contain collinear qualities.

## 8

CLASSIFICATION

Classification is a broad umbrella term for algorithms that generate category predictions, such as recommender systems that predict user preferences, image processing for facial recognition, and clustering analysis for conducting market research and customer profiling. Different from regression analysis, classification is used for predicting discrete categories rather than continuous values.

Classification models tend to be more common in industry than regression analysis. According to experienced data practitioner, Tavish Srivastava, Vice President of Digital Marketing and Analytics at Citi Bank, "In the four years of my data science career I have built more than 80% classification models and just 15-20% regression models. These ratios can be more or less generalized throughout the industry."[29]

Srivastava reasons that because most analytical problems involve forming a decision, classification helps to produce what he terms an *implementation roadmap*. In the case of an email spam detection system, the email client applies a classification algorithm to determine whether an incoming email is "spam" or "non-spam," which can be linked to a designated action rather than feeding back an index number quantifying the level of possible malice.

---

[29] Tavish Srivastava, "Introduction to k-Nearest Neighbors: Simplified," *Analytics Vidhya*, March 27 2018,
https://www.analyticsvidhya.com/blog/2018/03/introduction-k-neighbours-algorithm-clustering/

Examples of classification algorithms include decision trees, Bayes' classifier, and logistic regression.

Logistic Regression

Whereas linear, non-linear, and exponential regression analysis quantify the relationship between variables to predict a continuous output, logistic regression works as a classification technique to predict discrete classes. Hence, rather than quantify how much a customer will spend over a given period of time, logistic regression is used to qualify whether the customer is a new customer or a returning customer. There are thus two discrete possible outputs: **new customer** or **returning customer**.

Many people ask why logistic regression is named "regression" given it's used for classification and not for regression? The answer is that although its use case is classification, logistic regression is related to the regression family of algorithms because it predicts outcomes based on the correlation between continuous input variables. It's just that these relationships are assigned a discrete output value rather than a numerical output as is the case with linear regression.

Similar to linear regression, logistic regression measures the mathematical relationship between a dependent variable and its independent variables, but it then adds what's called a Sigmoid function to convert the relationship into an expression of probability between 0 and 1.0. A value of 0 represents no chance of occurring, whereas 1 represents a certain chance of occurring.

The degree of probability for values located between 0 and 1 can be calculated according to how close they rest to 0 (impossible) and 1 (certain possibility). The value 0.75, for example, would be considered a probable possibility or expressed as a 75% possibility.

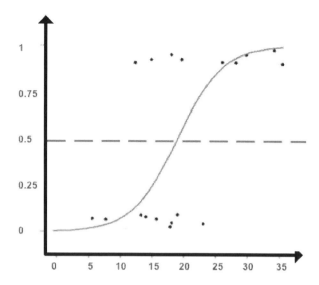

Figure 11: A Sigmoid function used to find the probability of an outcome

Based on the found probabilities of the independent variables, logistic regression assigns each data point to a discrete class. In the case of binary classification (shown in Figure 11), the cut-off line to classify data points is 0.5. Data points that record a value above 0.5 are classified as Class A, and data points below 0.5 are classified as Class B. Data points that record a result of precisely 0.5 are unclassifiable but such instances are rare due to the mathematical component of the Sigmoid function.

Strengths

+ This algorithm is fast to run and transparent in terms of how it produces a given output.

+ Logistic regression excels at binary classification, where there are only two potential outcomes, i.e. pregnant and non-pregnant.

Weaknesses

- Unfortunately, logistic regression is sensitive to outliers (data points that diverge from common patterns).

- Logistic regression is less accurate at analyzing a large number of inputs.

## 9

CLUSTERING

One of the core challenges of classification is categorizing data points without the knowledge of existing categories. This is true of fraud detection systems, where categories of attacks are constantly evolving and the culprits are adept at disguising their intentions. Spam email, too, isn't politely labeled as "spam" by the malicious bot sending suspicious mail to your email client.

One approach to solve this problem is to use a technique called *clustering analysis*. This technique is used to categorize data points into natural groupings in the absence of any predefined classes. Based on commonalities between variables, clustering analysis groups data points that possess a strong natural resemblance, which creates new classes/categories that can be used for category identification and further analysis.

A common example of clustering is finding customers that share similar purchasing patterns. By identifying a cluster of customers that share purchasing preferences, such as time of purchase and seasonal factors, you can make better decisions regarding which products to recommend via click ad banners and customized email campaigns.

In the music industry, clustering techniques are used to find similar beats by computing similarities in music composition between music titles. Songs that have been found to resemble each other in musical composition (omitting the analysis of lyrics) include *When Love Takes Over* by David Guetta and *Clocks* by

Coldplay, and *Why Don't You Get A Job?* by The Offspring and *Ob La Di Ob La Da* by The Beatles. By singling out natural groupings of song titles, music hosting services like Spotify can play relevant songs to users unrestrained by the traditional labels of artist, album, year of make, and genre.

Clustering analysis algorithms including *k*-means clustering and nearest neighbors are often used in both data mining and machine learning.

Nearest Neighbors

The nearest neighbors technique forms clusters by merging a known data point with one or more nearby data points. Using this technique, we can find similar types of cars or real estate properties by linking one or more known data points to nearby data points. For instance, if we know that one buyer holds a preference for a recently sold house located within 20 miles of the city center with three bedrooms and one bathroom, we can use the knowledge from this known data point to find other nearby data points based on overall proximity to those three variables.

k-means Clustering

Distinct from the previous technique, *k*-means clustering isolates clusters without relying on upfront knowledge of what it's predicting and isn't guided by a known starting point. This technique is useful for cases where you have no knowledge of an existing category but wish to find new unidentified groupings.

In practice, the dataset is split into *k* number of clusters, where *k* represents the number of clusters you wish to create. Setting *k* to "3," for example, splits the data into three clusters. To split data into clusters, each cluster is assigned a centroid, which is a data point that forms the epicenter of an individual cluster. Centroids can be chosen at random, which means you can nominate any data point on the scatterplot to assume the centroid role. The remaining data points on the scatterplot are then assigned to the closest centroid by measuring the Euclidean distance (straight-line distance between two points).

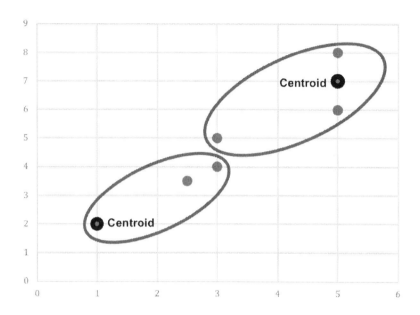

Figure 12: Two clusters are formed after calculating the Euclidean distance of the data points to the centroids

After all remaining data points have been assigned to a centroid, the next step is to aggregate the mean x and y values for each cluster.

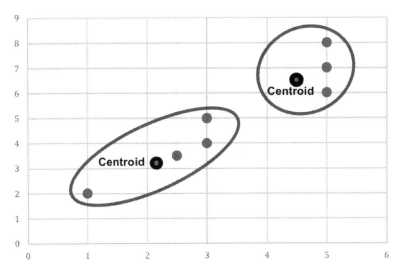

Figure 13: The centroid coordinates for each cluster are updated to reflect the cluster's mean value. As one data point has switched from the right cluster to the left cluster, the centroids of both clusters need to be updated.

You next take the mean x and y values of each cluster and plug in those values to update your centroid coordinates. This will most likely result in a change to your centroids' location. The total number of clusters, however, will remain the same. You are not creating new clusters, but rather updating their position on the scatterplot. Like musical chairs, the remaining data points rush to the closest centroid to form *k* number of clusters. The previous step is repeated should any data point switch clusters with the changing of centroids. This means, again, calculating the mean value and updating the x and y values of each centroid to reflect the average coordinates of all data points contained in each cluster.

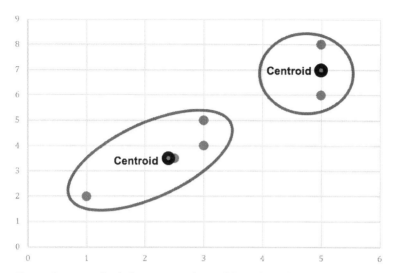

Figure 14: Two final clusters are formed based on the updated centroids for each cluster

The *k*-means clustering algorithm usually requires several iterations to find an ideal solution and reaches its conclusion when none of the data points switch clusters after an update in centroid coordinates.

A useful example of *k*-means clustering can be found on Nate Silver's blog FiveThirtyEight.com, which clusters the performance of players at the Men's FIFA World Cup.

In summary, *k*-means clustering analysis is useful when you already have an indication of how many groups exist in the dataset and you want to check how these groups look, or in situations when you don't know how many groups exist and you want the algorithm to produce an estimate.

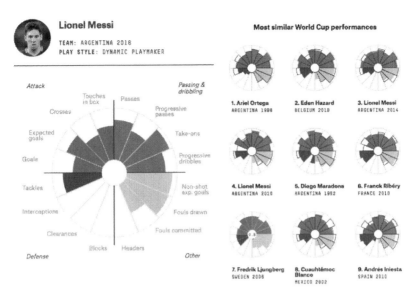

Figure 15: Lionel Messi versus World Cup player performances from 1966 to 2018.
Source: https://projects.fivethirtyeight.com/world-cup-comparisons/

Strengths

+ Clustering analysis is easy to interpret and visualize in the case of k-means clustering.

+ Clustering techniques are especially useful for finding new relationships in the form of unsupervised learning and for simplifying complex data.

Weaknesses

- Clustering techniques struggle to differentiate between relevant and irrelevant variables and poor variable selection has an adverse effect on the model's relevancy.

- These techniques can rely on human judgment, i.e. specifying the number k clusters in the case of k-means clustering, and there are no existing categories to benchmark the accuracy of the predictions.

## 10

ASSOCIATION ANALYSIS & SEQUENCE MINING

Association analysis is a rule-based method for discovering interesting relations between variables in large datasets. Known also as *market basket analysis*, this family of algorithms is often used by supermarkets and retail outlets to find associations between products using point-of-sale system data.

For instance, customers that buy nori (sheets of seaweed used for making sushi), rice, and soy sauce, are probably likely to buy other associated products such as salmon, cucumber, and wasabi. Association analysis seeks to tease out these associations as the basis for informing a variety of decisions including recommending products to users, organizing in-store product placement, and setting a pricing strategy to cross-market and cross-sell related items.

Association analysis is an example of unsupervised learning and is a common data mining technique. Unlike supervised learning, where independent variables are analyzed against an existing dependent variable, association analysis analyzes the relationship between independent variables to find a new output. An example of an association rule might be that a customer purchasing **bananas** and **cereal** is also likely to purchase **milk**.

The independent variables are also categorical/discrete rather than numeric/continuous, such as a product type (i.e. banana), film (i.e. The Matrix) or book (i.e. Sapiens: A Brief History of Humankind).

Frequent Itemsets & Support

Association analysis starts with constructing what's called *frequent itemsets*, which is a combination of items that regularly appear together. The combination could be one item with another item or it could be a combination of two or more items with one or more other items. From here, you can calculate an index number called *support* that indicates how often these items appear together.

Please note that in notation, "support" and "itemset" are expressed as "SUPP" and "X" respectively. Support (SUPP) can be calculated by dividing X by T, where X is how often the itemset appears in the data and T is your total number of transactions or data points. For example, if wasabi only features once in five transactions, then the support for wasabi is $1/5 = 0.2$.

 It's important to note that not all association rules are strong or useful, especially rules that occur infrequently and which lead to few sales or low customer uptake. Instead, the goal is to discover rules that are frequent and useful for decision-making. To save time and to concentrate on items with higher support, you can choose to set a minimum level known as *minimal support* or *minsup* (i.e. itemsets that account for 30% of total transactions), which will enable you to ignore low-level cases of support.

After finding frequent itemsets with minimal support, the next step is to turn each combination into a rule, i.e., Onions + Bread Buns > Hamburger Meat. This process is called *rule generation* and constitutes a collection of if/then statements. Rule generation also enables you to calculate *confidence,* which is a measure of accuracy or how often the rule holds true. For example, all transactions containing onions (A) and bread buns (A) with hamburger meat (B) is 0.3. This means that when a customer buys onions and bread buns, hamburger meat is also bought in 30% of cases.

The confidence level for each rule is important as it might not be practical for the organization to act on and implement every rule that meets minimum support. Confidence levels therefore help organizations to focus on implementing changes based on rules that contain the most upside for potential gain. Equally, confidence levels can help the organization to order the prioritization of implementing association rules over an extended period of time.

Numerous algorithms can be applied to perform association analysis. Below is a list of the most common techniques:

- Apriori
- Eclat (equivalence class transformations)
- FP-growth (frequent pattern)
- RElim (recursive elimination)
- SaM (split and merge)
- JIM (Jaccard itemset mining)

Apriori is generally the most popular algorithm for association analysis and follows a bottom-up approach to calculate support for itemsets one item at a time. It finds the support of one item (how common that item is in the dataset) and determines whether there is support for that item. If the support is less than the designated minimum support (minsup), the observed item is ignored. Apriori will then move on to the next item and evaluate the minsup value and determine whether it should hold on to the item or ignore it and move on. After the algorithm has evaluated all single-item itemsets, it will transition to processing two-item itemsets, then three-item combinations, and so on, to generate successively longer itemsets that meet minimum support at each level of the itemset.

Inversely, this technique has a "downward closure property" where subtracting items from a large frequent itemset continues to yield a frequent itemset with minimum support. This means that subsets of an Apriori frequent itemset are also frequent itemsets. For instance, if A, B, C, D, E is a frequent itemset, then any subset such as (A, B, C, D) or (C, D) is also a frequent itemset.

However, because the minsup criteria is applied to every itemset, each new combination requires a scan through the dataset to determine its minimum support, and this translates to a high cost in computational resources. While the minsup value can help to limit the computations needed to generate association rules, machine processing expands exponentially with each round of analysis, which makes this method inefficient at analyzing large datasets.

A popular alternative for working with larger datasets is the Eclat algorithm. Similar to Apriori, Eclat calculates the support for a single itemset, but, when and if the minsup value is reached, it directly adds an additional item (now a two-item itemset). Thus, unlike Apriori which processes all single items first, Eclat adds as many items to the original item as possible, until it fails to reach the set minsup. This approach is faster and takes up less computation and memory. The trade-off, though, is that the itemsets generated are often long and difficult to manipulate once assembled.

Apriori Method Example

Let's now take a look at the Apriori method in practice using the following table containing e-commerce transactions among nine customers.

Transactions				
Customer 1	Air Pods	Nike trainers	Cannon camera	iPhone
Customer 2	Samsung Galaxy	Nike trainers	Energy drink	
Customer 3	iPhone	Air Pods	Nike trainers	Energy drink
Customer 4	iPhone	Energy drink		
Customer 5	iPhone	Air Pods	Nike trainers	
Customer 6	iPhone	Air Pods		
Customer 7	Nike trainers	Energy drink		
Customer 8	Samsung Galaxy	Adidas trainers		
Customer 9	Energy drink	Air Pods	Nike trainers	

Table 12: All e-commerce transactions

First, let's look at the single itemsets to see how often each item appears in a transaction.

1-itemsets	Frequency
Air Pods	5
Nike trainers	6
Cannon camera	1
iPhone	5
Samsung Galaxy	2
Energy drink	5
Adidas trainers	1

Table 13: Frequency of each individual item

If we set minsup to 0.3, we need an item to appear in at least three of the nine transactions (3/9). Based on this condition, the 1-itemsets we can analyze are: Air Pods, Nike trainers, iPhone, and Energy drink. The remaining three items (Canon camera, Samsung Galaxy and Adidas trainers) fail to reach minimum support and are therefore ignored by the Apriori method.

Let's now use these four frequent items to create 2-itemsets.

2-itemsets	Frequency
Air Pods + iPhone	4
Air Pods + Nike trainers	4
Air Pods + Energy drink	2
iPhone + Nike trainers	3
iPhone + Energy drink	2
Nike trainers + Energy drink	4

Table 14: Frequency of 2-itemsets

Using the same minsup criteria as before (0.3), **Air Pods + Energy drink** (2) and **iPhone + Energy drink** (2) don't qualify as a frequent itemset as they appear in less than 3/9 transactions. Note also that as Samsung phone, Canon camera, and Adidas shoes do not meet minimum support, we cannot add them to a 2-itemset combination.

Let's next look at the 3-itemsets.

3-itemsets	Frequency
Air Pods + iPhone + Nike trainers	3
Air Pods + iPhone + Energy drink	1
Air Pods + Nike trainers + Energy drink	1
iPhone + Nike trainers + Energy drink	2

Table 15: Frequency of 3-itemsets

At this round, only **Air Pods + iPhone + Nike trainers** achieve the minsup criteria of 0.3 (3/9=0.33), and the other three rules must be ignored.

Using our only 3-itemset, we can generate rules and their individual confidence levels. Confidence is calculated by dividing the frequency of the 3-itemset by the frequency of its own 2-itemset.

1)

Air Pods + iPhone + Nike trainers = 3

Air Pods + iPhone = 4

3/4 = 75%

Thus, customers who purchase **Air Pods + iPhone** have a confidence level of 75% (3/4) of purchasing Nike trainers.

2)

Air Pods + iPhone + Nike trainers = 3

Air Pods + Nike trainers = 4

3/4 = 75%

Customers who purchase **Air Pods + Nike trainers** likewise have a confidence level of 75% (3/4) of purchasing an **iPhone**.

3)

Air Pods + iPhone + Nike trainers = 3

iPhone + Nike trainers = 3

3/3 = 100%

Customers who purchase **iPhone + Nike trainers** always (3/3) purchase **Air Pods** as well.

Next, let's see if we can build a 4-item set using all the items that meet the minimum of 0.3 in support.

4-itemsets	Frequency
Air Pods + iPhone + Nike trainers + Energy drink	1

Table 16: Frequency of the failed 4-itemset

This time, unfortunately, there is insufficient support (1/9=0.11) to build a frequent itemset (the minimum is 0.3) consisting of four items.

Sequence Mining

Similar and yet different from association analysis, sequence mining is a method of identifying repeated sequences in a dataset. This technique can be applied to various scenarios, such as instructing a person what to do or predicting what will transpire next. Another example of sequence mining is found in text analysis, where a set of sentences, words, letters, or syllables from a text can be viewed as a sequence, also known as an *n-gram*.

Sequence mining is similar to association analysis in terms of predicting if x occurs then z and y are also likely to occur. The difference, though, with sequence mining is that the order of the events is important. In association analysis, it doesn't matter if the combination is "x, y, and z," or "z, y, and x," whereas in sequence mining the precise order does matter.

A number of algorithms can be applied to conduct sequence mining, including:

- GSP (Generalized Sequential Patterns)
- SPADE (Sequential Pattern Discovery using Equivalence)
- FreeSpan
- HMM (Hidden Markov Model)

Perhaps the most common method for sequence mining is Generalized Sequential Patterns (GSP). Although similar to Apriori in its workflow, GSP analyzes the order of events, which could be ordinal or temporal. Temporal refers to the state of time while ordinal refers to the logical progression of categories, i.e., elementary school > middle school > senior school, or single > engaged > married. Like Apriori, GSP has to complete many passes over the data to finalize its groupings, which can be slow and computationally expensive to process.

Using the earlier dataset (now ordered by month), we can use the GSP approach to analyze the sequence of purchases.

	Jan	Feb	March	April
Customer 1	Air Pods	Nike trainers	Cannon camera	iPhone
Customer 2	Samsung Galaxy	Nike trainers	Energy drink	
Customer 3	iPhone	Air Pods	Nike trainers	Energy drink
Customer 4	iPhone	Energy drink		
Customer 5	iPhone	Air Pods	Nike trainers	
Customer 6	iPhone	Air Pods		
Customer 7	Nike trainers	Energy drink		
Customer 8	Samsung Galaxy	Adidas trainers		
Customer 9	Energy drink	Air Pods	Nike trainers	

Table 17: All e-commerce transactions by month

Like association analysis, sequence mining uses a minimum support criteria to focus on frequent patterns as well as a confidence level to inform decision-making and prioritize implementation. Using a minsup of 0.3 (3/9), we can examine the same four product items used in the previous example to create our frequent itemsets: Air Pods, iPhone, Nike trainers & Energy drink.

2-itemsets	Frequency
Air Pods + iPhone	0
Air Pods + Nike trainers	4
Air Pods + Energy drink	0
iPhone + Nike trainers	0
iPhone + Energy drink	1
iPhone + Air Pods	3
Nike trainers + Air Pods	1
Nike trainers + iPhone	0
Nike trainers + Energy drink	3
Energy drink + Air Pods	1
Energy drink + iPhone	0
Energy drink + Nike trainers	0

Table 18: Frequency of sequential 2-itemsets

Air Pods + Nike trainers (4), **iPhone + Air Pods** (3), and **Nike trainers + Energy drink** (3) meet the minsup criteria of 0.3 (3/9) for a frequent 2-itemset. Let's now look at potential 3-itemsets.

3-itemsets	Frequency
Air Pods + Nike trainers + iPhone	0
Air Pods + Nike trainers + Energy drink	1
iPhone + Air Pods + Nike trainers	2
iPhone + Aid Pods + Energy drink	0
Nike trainers + Energy drink + Air Pods	0
Nike trainers + Energy drink + iPhone	0

Table 19: Frequency of sequential 3-itemsets

At this round, no itemsets qualify as frequent (3/9). However, using our three frequent 2-itemsets, we can generate the following rules and confidence levels.

1)

Air Pods + Nike trainers = 4

Air Pods = 5

4/5 = 80%

Customers who purchase **Air Pods** have a confidence of 80% (4/5) of purchasing **Nike trainers** as their next item.

2)

iPhone + Air Pods = 3

iPhone = 5

3/5 = 60%

Customers who purchase an **iPhone** have a confidence of 60% (3/5) of purchasing **Air Pods** as their next item.

3)

Nike trainers + Energy drink = 3

Nike trainers = 6

3/6 = 50%

Customers who purchase **Nike trainers** have a confidence of 50% (3/6) of purchasing an **Energy drink** next.

Strengths

+ Association analysis and sequence mining are easy to understand. They also provide confidence levels to aid decision-making regarding which combinations to prioritize.

+ Both techniques are excellent for examining categorical/discrete input variables.

Weaknesses

- While suitable for offline retail scenarios, association analysis does not factor in user preferences (i.e. likes and ratings), which are pervasive and precious in the online world. Other more comprehensive techniques, such as collaborative-based filtering and content filtering, are therefore preferred for recommending online items.

## 11

NATURAL LANGUAGE PROCESSING

Natural language processing (NLP) is a unique and specialized subfield of machine learning inspired by linguistics—the study of language and semantics. Intended for parsing text in databases using coding rules systems, NLP was originally used for analyzing sentence construction and language. Over time, these techniques merged with common algorithms from the machine learning world to evolve into a new powerful method of computational linguistics.

Endorsed by the ubiquity and value of unstructured data contained in emails, chat logs, web pages, social media posts, support tickets, and survey responses, NLP has developed into a highly promising field of work. Today, a myriad of applications including Siri, Google Assistant, and Facebook use NLP techniques for text parsing, which includes voice recognition (using speech-to-text conversion) and retrieving text information from user search queries.

Given the nuances and complexity of analyzing unstructured data in the form of spoken and written language, extracting insight from a text can be a challenging and imprecise method. NLP is therefore a much more ambiguous subfield of analysis than association analysis, regression, and other domains of classification. It is also unique from other common algorithm categories because the data is unstructured rather than structured—making it less compatible with traditional algorithms.

In practice, NLP is commonly assigned to classification tasks such as named entity recognition (finding names or dates), sentiment analysis, and tagging blobs of text. In NLP, stand-alone items of text are referred to as a *document*. Examples include a news item, blog post, email message, comment, customer support ticket, Tweet, as well as other forms of text-based records. Multiple documents can also be organized into a corpus that can be used as training data for language analysis. Examples of a corpus include chat archives, a compilation of Shakespeare's writings, or news articles compiled on a topic that can be used for targeted analysis.

Individual documents can be broken into smaller bits known as *tokens*, which are individual words and punctuation symbols, including emoticons, which attribute or modify the meaning of a sentence.

Lastly, NLP is sequenced-based, meaning that the position of words modifies the interpretation of other words and overall grammatical structure.

Corpus	Tokens	Vocabulary Size
Switchboard phone conversations	2.4 million	20,000
Shakespeare	884,000	31,000
Google N-grams	1 trillion	12 million

Table 20: Corpus examples, *Source: Dan Jurafsky & Christopher Manning, Word Tokenization, Natural Language Processing, YouTube*

The goal of NLP is to pull apart the document's sentence structure to determine the role of each token. This begins with text pre-processing (i.e. stripping the capitalization of words), tokenization (chopping up the document into a list of words), and stemming (i.e. converting "writer" into "write"). The pre-processing stage may also involve removing basic grammatical elements from the document such as stop words (i.e. "the", "a", and "an"). This allows the algorithm to run faster using less data and is useful for simple tasks such as named entity recognition and parsing large amounts of text.

Next, it's important to note the technical distinction between *syntax analysis* and *semantic analysis*. Syntax refers to sentence structure, i.e. does a sentence end with a question mark, or are words capitalized? Using word frequency, named entity recognition, and other techniques, syntax analysis is used to break down a sentence's structure and components. Semantics, meanwhile, represents the fundamental intent or meaning attached to the text. Understanding the semantics of a text enables the model to perform language translation or answer questions via a chatbox/voice recognition assistant. Machine translation, for example, doesn't rely solely on parsing syntax to directly translate a sentence into a different language. The machine needs to decode what has been said before re-expressing the intent of the sentence in another language. Semantic analysis is also referred to as *natural language understanding* in order to distinguish it from *syntax analysis* and *general natural language processing* that analyze the text at a lower level of comprehension.

The following section provides a summary of key NLP methods and a practical introduction to the term frequency-inverse document frequency (tf–idf) method.

Stemming

Stemming is used for pre-processing and involves stripping words to their core meaning. This includes removing past/present stems by removing "ed" or "ing" or other modifiers such as "globalized," "globalism," and "globally" to return the stem "global." Google, for example, uses stemming to chop off word endings to improve efficiency and reduce word variation for analyzing Google search requests.

Edit Distance

Edit distance examines the difference between words. "Data" and "date," for example, are differentiated by one letter, which gives them an edit distance of 1. This simple technique underwrites spellcheck systems and word suggestions for online search queries.

Named Entity Recognition

As a vital part of NLP, named entity recognition picks out salient parts of text such as *what* (concert), *where* (Madison Square Garden), and *who* (college friends) and plays an essential role in chat-box and other online assistant applications.

Intent Abstraction

Another vital component of NLP is intent abstraction. This technique is similar to named entity recognition but parses a sentence to perform an action such as adding information to a database, calendar, or social media monitoring application.

Relationship Extraction

Relationship extraction is used to extract semantic elements that relate to other elements in a sentence, such as "**Steve Jobs** and **Steve Wozniak** created **Apple.**"

tf–idf

Term frequency-inverse document frequency or tf–idf is a numerical statistic of how important a word is to a document and its corpus. The tf–idf value reflects the frequency of a word in a document and the number of documents in the corpus containing that word.

In order to offset the bias of frequently used words like "the" and "a" in any given document, tf–idf uses a weighting system to increase the weight of unique terms that appear less frequently. The tf–idf technique is often used as a weighting factor in searches of information retrieval and text mining and is said to be used in 83% of text-based recommender systems in digital libraries.[30]

The formula for term frequency-inverse document frequency is broken down as follows:

Term Frequency:

$tf_{x,y}$ = The number of occasions term x appears in a single document (y)

Inverse Document Frequency:

$\log(N/df_x)$ = The number of documents (N) containing term x

These two equations can then be added to produce the tf–idf formula:

$$tf_{x,y} \times \log \left(\frac{N}{df_x} \right)$$

Where:

x = term

y = a document

$tf_{x,y}$ = frequency of term x in document y

log = base 10 logarithm

N = total number of documents

df_x = number of documents containing term x

Suppose we have two documents that include the following terms:

---

[30] Corinna Breitinger, Bela Gipp, Stefan Langer, "Research-paper recommender systems: a literature survey," *International Journal on Digital Libraries,* July 26, 2015

Document 1		Document 2	
Term	Count	Term	Count
This	10	This	5
AI	10	AI	1
AlphaGo	4	David	4

Table 21: Sample documents

The TF (term frequency) for the word "AlphaGo" can be calculated as follows:

Document 1 tf: (AlphaGo, D1) = 4/24 (0.166)
Document 2 tf: (AlphaGo, D2) = 0/10 (0)

IDF (inverse document frequency) for "AlphaGo" is calculated as follows:
idf: log(2/1) = 0.301

Document 1 tf–idf: 0.166 × 0.301 = 0.05
Document 2 tf–idf: 0 × 0.301 = 0

Let's now find the tf–idf for another term, "this":

Document 1 tf: (this, D1) = 10/24 (0.416)
Document 2 tf: (this, D2) = 5/10 (0.5)32

idf: log(2/2) = 0

Document 1 tf–idf = 0.416 × 0 = 0
Document 2 tf–idf = 0.5 × 0 = 0

Based on the comparison of these two terms, tf–idf finds that the second term "this" (0) appears in all documents and is less informative than "AlphaGo" which appears prominently in only one document (0.05 in D1). AlphaGo is therefore a significant or important word in the context of Document 1.

Text Classification

As a fundamental NLP task, text classification involves assigning tags or categories to text relevant to its content and relies on using pre-labeled examples as training data. This technique is often used for binary classification tasks like classifying spam emails as well as more advanced tasks such as analyzing sentiment, topic labeling, and intent detection. Businesses often employ text classification to quickly label and redesign text into a structured format that is used for decision-making and automating processes, such as assessing the urgency of support tickets, finding relevant brand mentions, or flagging suspicious comments for manual review.

A popular text classification method is the *bag of words* approach, which converts text into a numeric structure using a defined dictionary of tokens. According to a dictionary with these words {machine, learning, deep, statistics, computer, science, hot}, the following sentence can be transformed into a numeric vector as follows.

Sample: "Machine learning is a promising field in computer science and a hot career prospect."
Numeric vector: (1, 1, 0, 0, 0, 0, 0, 1, 1, 0, 0, 1, 0, 0)

Vectors can then be compared with other vectors in order to carry out classification.

Sentiment Analysis

Sentiment analysis overlaps with text classification but focuses on the emotional intent of a document, such as a positive or negative product review. While analysis tends to be filtered to positive and negative emotions, sentiment analysis can be complex and catered to detecting sarcasm and identifying instances where the intent of words is contrary to their stand-alone meaning, such as "shockingly good."

Document Similarity

Lastly, document similarity finds relevant documents by analyzing the distance between documents based on semantic proximity or the description of similar concepts. As a technique, it is often used for information retrieval purposes such as finding identical or similar existing questions on Quora.com. A common approach to document similarity is to transform the target documents into tf–idf vectors and compute their similarity.

Strengths

+ NLP is an excellent choice for comprehending and analyzing text-based information.

+ NLP is one of the few reliable techniques for sorting and analyzing unstructured data.

Weaknesses

- Outputs will not always be precise. This is mainly due to the complicated nuance of language and the potential for human errors (i.e. input data sourced from second-language speakers or poor spelling/grammar). Human input may therefore be needed to verify the prediction, i.e. verification of Google language translations.

## 12

DATA VISUALIZATION

One of the common themes of business books and presentations today is the essential and almost souped-up role of marketing. Whether it's a sole trader or a massive online learning platform, businesses need a plan and strategy to promote what they have to offer. In some cases, the product or service speaks for itself. Here, we might think of Krispy Kreme in the early days of their global expansion or the mobile game Pokémon Go. Other products and services, meanwhile, lean on hundreds of millions of dollars to stretch their reach, paid by companies such as 20th Century Fox, Toyota, Samsung, Apple, and McDonald's.

The doppelganger or nearest neighbor to 'marketing' in the data science world is 'data visualization.' Similar to marketing, data visualization is a medium of communication ideal for persuading a general audience. Many white-hat marketing concepts, including visual design, storytelling, drawing attention to key points, and honesty hold true with data visualization. Equally, it's important to sidestep black-hat practices and manipulation for short-term gain.

Take for instance the bar plot chosen by the UK newspaper *The Times* to describe a lead in sales over its competitor *The Daily Telegraph*.

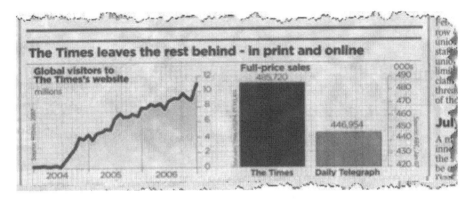

Figure 16: The Times leaves the rest behind – in print and online. Source: University of Kentucky

A closer look shows that the paper is ahead of its competitor by 10% in total sales, which is less impressive than the bar plot depicts. *The Times* is overextending its claim by manipulating and customizing the scale of the bar plot, which highlights the sales bracket of 420,000 to 490,000 rather than the maximum range of 0 to 490,000. As mentioned by Sarah Boslaugh in the book *Statistics in a Nutshell*, "choosing a misleading range is one of the time-honored ways to 'lie with statistics.'"

While this example is a classic case of manipulating how data is visualized, diverging from unique reporting styles isn't necessarily the solution. Data is highly nuanced and standard reporting templates used across organizations or even internal departments can obscure what the data is really saying. Ideally, reports should be tailored to the research question and trends the analyst is observing, while, of course, upholding the true intent of the data. As with marketing, data visualization is a strategic process. Each chart, annotation, and visual diagram must be scrutinized from the perspective of the target audience and harmonized with the integrity of the data. Techniques also vary greatly depending on the profile of the target audience.

Data visualization itself takes many forms including scorecards, dashboards, charts, and heatmaps, but all help to provide organizations with a better understanding of their operating environment. The dashboard format, for example, provides a canvas to juxtapose a number of relevant visualizations, including numeric and geospatial diagrams, as well as ample space to annotate key findings. Decision-makers often favor dashboards as it enables them to visualize the data while forcing the designer to curate the key findings to fit on a single page.

Explanatory Graphics and Exploratory Graphics

The utility of data visualization can be divided into two main use cases. The first is explanatory graphics, which is delivered to an external audience. The second use case is exploratory graphics, which is generated on-the-fly to aid internal understanding while analysis is in progress and the model is still in production mode.

The latter, exploratory graphics, helps data analysts to understand their data—especially new and complex datasets— and to gain a general sense of the patterns, including distribution, outliers and anomalies, linear relationships, and clusters of data points. This often takes the form of distribution tables, pairplots, and heatmaps to visualize common trends including correlation, as well as interactive visualization tools such as Tableau or code visualization libraries for generating different views of the data. As Mike Barlow writes in *Data Visualization: A New Language for Storytelling*, speed and the capacity to quickly compose different views of the data are key features of exploratory graphics.[31]

Explanatory graphics are produced during the last stage of production and help to explain your findings to stakeholders who aren't familiar with the data. The intended audience generally consists of people evaluating the outcome of your analysis, including senior decision-makers, data leads, product managers, partners, and customers, who may not be data experts.

---

[31] Mike Barlow, "Data Visualization: A New Language for Storytelling," *O'Reilly Media*, 2015.

Explanatory graphics should help place the findings and methods of analysis into context and highlight aspects of the data that are most relevant. As with the Arab saying, "no skill to understand it, mastery to write it," visualizations should be easy to interpret and especially for decision-makers with low data literacy.

In practical terms, this might mean using icons and images where possible, labeling charts and graphs with relevant information (such as a sudden spike in online traffic or a fall in revenue due to a seminal event), and keeping any jargon encased in titles and text boxes to a minimum.

Examples of Data Visualization

In this section, we will take a quick tour of the most common and useful methods of data visualization.

Line Charts

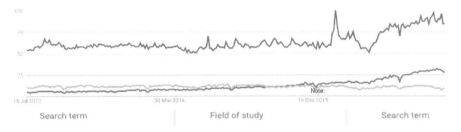

Figure 17: Google Trends keyword line chart

From Google Trends to the 6pm weather report, line charts help visualize changes in one variable against another, such as income across age brackets or search traffic plotted over time. Line charts are easy to interpret and work extremely well at describing trends over time.

Bar Charts and Histograms

Bar charts visualize data variables using vertical or horizontal bars and are ideal for visualizing discrete data with a limited number of categories. They are less flexible, though, at showing how variables impact other variables such as web traffic over a period of time.

Figure 18: Google Trends keyword average expressed in a bar chart

Histograms, as shown in Figure 19, are very similar to bar charts but don't contain a margin or a blank space between bars. This translates to more available space for visualizing multiple bars.

Figure 19: Google Trends keyword average expressed through a histogram

Bar Chart Races

You might have noticed that animated bar chart races have grown popular on YouTube and Instagram. These animated bar charts are great for showing the evolution of numerical data over time while also being extremely eye-catching.

Matt Navarra ✅
@MattNavarra

WOAH...!

Top 15 BEST global brands ranking for the last 19 years...

Watch big name tech companies take-over at the end!

h/t @Interbrand

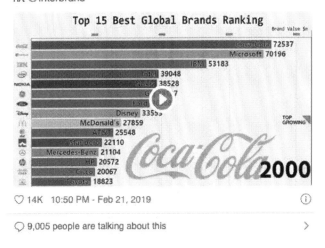

Top 15 Best Global Brands Ranking

Coca-Cola 72537
Microsoft 70196
IBM 53183
Intel 39048
Nokia 38528
Disney 3355?
McDonald's 27859
AT&T 25548
22110
Mercedes-Benz 21104
HP 20572
Cisco 20067
Toyota 18823

2000

♡ 14K   10:50 PM - Feb 21, 2019   ⓘ

💬 9,005 people are talking about this   ＞

Figure 20: Matt Narvarra's original Tweet in 2019.

Matt Navarra, a British digital media consultant who used to be the Director of Social Media at The Next Web, helped spread the trend after he shared the top 15 best global brands over the last 19 years. The tweet bounced around Twitter, racking up thousands of likes and retweets and hundreds of replies. In the same week, John Burn-Murdoch, a data visualization journalist at the Financial Times in London, tweeted out his code for making a bar chart race, which added even more awareness.

You can build your own bar chart race using time series data and software like Tableau or flourish.studio (https://app.flourish.studio/@flourish/bar-chart-race) which you can sign up and use for free.

Pie Charts

Pie charts represent variable values in proportion to other variable values. The larger the slice, the larger that variable is in relation to other variables. As with bar charts, pie charts are ideal for visualizing a limited number of categories and especially when there is a significant difference in proportions between categories.

Figure 21: Google Trends keyword average expressed with a pie chart

Scatterplots

The scatterplot is used for plotting quantifiable relationships between continuous variables and conveying information about the relationship between those variables, such as identifying outliers and anomalies, data variance, natural groups, and shape (i.e. linear, non-linear). Looking at raw data, it's often difficult to spot these trends—especially linear relationships between variables—which explains why data analysts rely on scatterplots to gain a general sense of relationships in the data.

Scatterplots can be used in a variety of ways, including regression and clustering analysis. Scatterplots can be generated in one, two (bivariant), three, and four dimensions but two and three dimensions are most common.

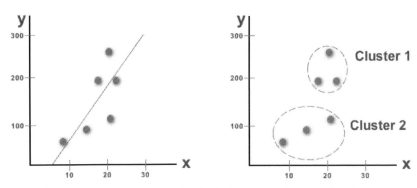

Figure 22: Clustering and regression techniques on a 2-D scatterplot

Each data point on the plot corresponds to one instance from the dataset, described by a set of coordinates (x, y). When analyzing the relationship between an independent and dependent variable in regression analysis, the former is plotted on the x-axis (horizontal) and the latter on the y-axis (vertical). In other situations, it doesn't matter which variable is plotted on which axis.

Box Plots
The box plot, also known as the box-and-whiskers plot, is used for summarizing and displaying the distribution of a set of continuous data. Box plots are useful for visualizing outliers, describing symmetry, and conveying how tightly the data is grouped. Box plots display the distribution of data according to the minimum, first quartile (Q1), median (Q2), third quartile (Q3), and maximum of the data.

Quartile	Explanation
First quartile (25th percentile)	Separates the lowest 25% of the data from the highest 75%
Second quartile (50th percentile)	Interquartile range from the 25th to the 75th percentile (median)
Third quartile (75th percentile)	Separates the highest 25% of the data from the lowest 75%

Table 22: Explanation of quartiles

The first quartile (Q_1) is defined as the section between the minimum and the median of the dataset. The median is the second quartile (Q_2), which represents the interquartile range. This section is calculated as the difference between the 75th and 25th percentile values and **constitutes** the middle 50% of the dataset. The interquartile range is important because it is less influenced by extreme values than the full range of the dataset. The third quartile (Q_3) is the section between the median and the maximum of the dataset.

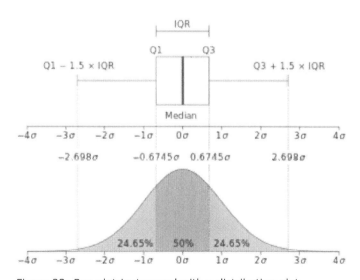

Figure 23: Box plot juxtaposed with a distribution plot

Box plots, shown at the top of Figure 23 and again in Figure 24, resemble a rectangle box. The box contains the second quartile/median, and the two lines (called whiskers) extending vertically from the box represent the first and third quartile respectively. Outliers that fall between the minimum and the first quartile or the maximum and the third quartile can be plotted as individual points outside the whiskers.

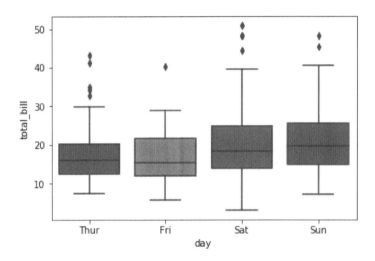

Figure 24: Example of box plots

Lastly, the horizontal line inside the rectangle box notes the symmetry of the data. If the box is symmetric with a line down the middle, it means that the data follows a normal distribution. If the box is not symmetric it means the data is skewed.

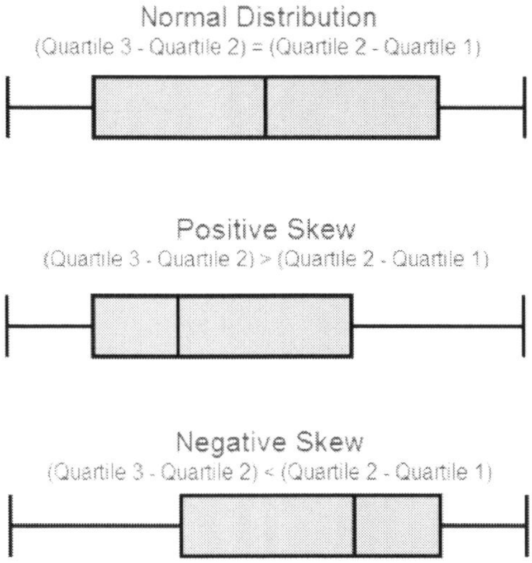

Normal Distribution
(Quartile 3 - Quartile 2) = (Quartile 2 - Quartile 1)

Positive Skew
(Quartile 3 - Quartile 2) > (Quartile 2 - Quartile 1)

Negative Skew
(Quartile 3 - Quartile 2) < (Quartile 2 - Quartile 1)

Figure 25: Distribution of normal distribution, positive skew, and negative skew.
Source: http://datapigtechnologies.com

Violin Plots

Violin plots also visualize the variance of the data but with slightly more detail. The downside is that violin plots are less often used compared to box plots, which means they might not be as suitable for explanatory graphics.

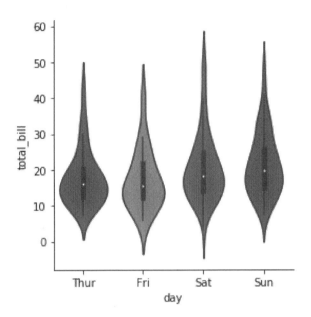

Figure 26: Example of violin plots

Rug Plots

Rug plots visualize the distribution of a single variable by plotting data along an axis, often in the form of a one-dimensional scatterplot or histogram. Rug plots are useful for exploratory graphics as they help the user gain a general understanding of spread within the data.

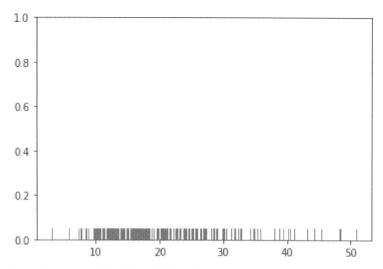

Figure 27: A rug plot plotted along the x-axis of a 2-D scatterplot

Rug plots owe their name to their common placement along the x-axis and/or y-axis of a two-dimensional scatterplot, which looks like tassels skirting the edges of a rectangular "rug."

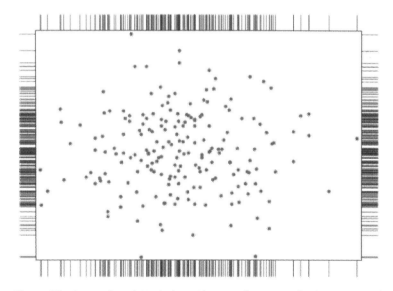

Figure 28: A rug plot plotted along the x and y-axes of a 2-D scatterplot

Pairplots

Pairplots are used in exploratory graphics as a quick way to understand patterns between variables. Pairplots take the form of a grid of plots that display selected variables from the dataset and can be generated as 2-D or 3-D plots. Pairplots can also be a great jumping-off point for determining types of regression analysis to use and assessing which independent variables are correlated.

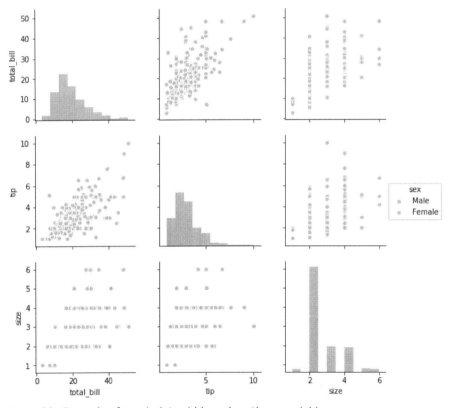

Figure 29: Example of a pairplot grid based on three variables

When plotted against another variable (multivariant), the visualization takes the form of a scatterplot, and when plotted against the same variable (univariant), a simple histogram/bar plot is applied, as shown in Figure 29.

Heatmaps

Heatmaps are often used by data scientists for exploratory graphics. Correlation values between variables are represented as colors contained inside a matrix, with variables represented as both columns and rows.

	total_bill	tip	size
total_bill	1.000000	0.675734	0.598315
tip	0.675734	1.000000	0.489299
size	0.598315	0.489299	1.000000

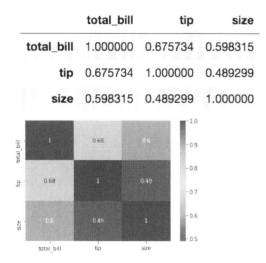

Figure 30: Example of a heatmap

Aesthetic Design

In the penultimate section of this chapter, we discuss the aesthetic design of explanatory graphics, beginning with color.

While color provides visual appeal, an excessive number of colors can be overwhelming. Unless you need to visualize a high number of clusters or objects, it's better to limit visualizations to seven colors or less. This will also help to ensure your visualizations look professional.

If your organization has a set color palette for visual branding purposes, then it makes sense to utilize this guide and especially if your visualizations are to be viewed by customers and shared on social media. If you are choosing a palette, you can find free resources like Adobe Color CC (https://color.adobe.com/create/color-wheel/) with an interactive color wheel to help you customize and select color combinations.

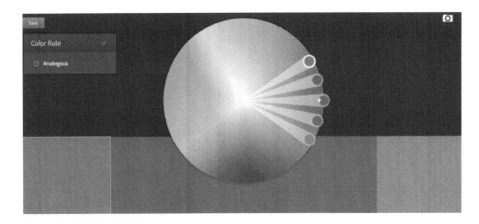

Figure 31: Adobe Color CC wheel

It's important to pick distinctive colors, especially if you need to distinguish a high number of clusters. One tool you can use is Hue (http://tools.medialab.sciences-po.fr/iwanthue/) which generates color schemes for data scientists.

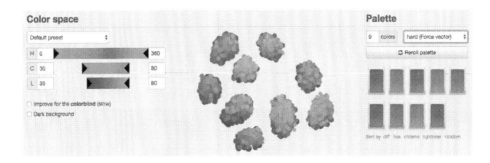

Figure 32: Hue, color schemes for data scientists

Another often overlooked consideration is approximately 1 in 12 men (8%) and 1 in 200 (0.5%) women are classed as colorblind.[32]

Tools like Hue and ColorBrewer (http://colorbrewer2.org/) provide a filter that lets you select from palettes pre-tested for color blindness.

Lastly, you may need to pay attention to cultural contexts when designing and presenting your data. In East Asia, for example, red is associated with "good fortune" and "prosperity." Stock price gains are therefore displayed in red and falls in green. This is the opposite color scheme for stock price movements in the West, where green is associated as positive. Avoiding red and green to visualize gains and losses is one solution to neutralize potential confusion.

Data Visualization Tools

In this final section, we'll review three popular visualization tools used by data practitioners, which come with built-in routines to create various types of charts and graphs.

Microsoft Power BI

Branded as a business intelligence[33] (BI) tool, Microsoft Power BI is a popular software program for data visualization.

Business intelligence reports and tools were traditionally dominated by Oracle, IBM, SAP, and, of course, Microsoft, and their offerings were mostly confined to large enterprise customers that paid for reports and visualizations requested by business managers. Microsoft broke the status quo in the mid-1990s with the release of Excel, which for the first time, enabled users to analyze their own data in an offline setting and define the general appearance of spreadsheets, including fonts, character attributes, and cells. In addition, it introduced extensive graphing capabilities that laid the foundation for Power BI.

---

[32] "Colour Blindness," *colourblindnessawareness.org*, viewed January 20 2019, http://www.colourblindawareness.org/colour-blindness/.
[33] Business intelligence refers to technology-driven processes for analyzing data and presenting actionable information to inform business decisions.

Released to the general public in 2015, Power BI incorporates many of Excel's existing features but with more attention to data visualization. The first version of Power BI included numerous Microsoft add-ons such as Power Query, Power Pivot, and Power View. Microsoft later added new features such as Questions and Answers, additional sharing options, and advanced security settings.

Today, Power BI enables you to connect to hundreds of data sources (including MailChimp, Google Analytics, CSV files, Excel workbooks, Github, Salesforce, Azure SQL Server, etc.), create live dashboards and reports, and share your visualizations across a range of platforms.

One of the comparative advantages of using Power BI is the many options available for sharing visualizations and reports to end-users. This includes export options for Microsoft PowerPoint and Microsoft SharePoint, web authoring options, scannable QR (quick response) codes for access to graphics, and the ability to share visualizations inside the Power BI iPad app. In addition, users can create dashboards in a private group, approve editors and contributors, and choose from a variety of security options, including where data is hosted.

The other advantage of Power BI is the familiarity of its interface. For many people, Excel was their first foray into manipulating data and business intelligence, and they are familiar with the layout and user experience of Microsoft software.

If you need help using Power BI, there are hundreds of Power BI meetups hosted around the world, and answers can be found online at https://community.powerbi.com/.

Tableau

Tableau provides the next step up in data visualization. Tableau has built its business model on data visualization and the results show as few software solutions compare with Tableau in terms of product support, online community, and the depth of tools provided.

Like Power BI, Tableau is a stand-alone software program and supports a range of visualization techniques including charts, graphs, maps, and other visualization options. Tableau is also regarded as more interactive than Power BI as it allows users to ask deeper questions of their data and discover new insight rather than just adding an aesthetic coat to the data. The downside is that Tableau is more expensive than Power BI and other solutions on the market.

If you find yourself weighing up between Power BI and Tableau, Encore Business Solutions have created a free tool to generate a recommendation for your specific use case. Link: https://www.encorebusiness.com/bi-recommendation-tool/

Programming Languages and Third-party Libraries

While standalone software solutions like Power BI and Tableau are excellent for creating professional and shareable visualizations, there are powerful and flexible options available directly within your code notebook. Using programming languages like Python and R and special data visualization code libraries, you can execute advanced visualizations with minimal code and export them as an image. Best of all, there is no cost for generating your own visualizations using code.

Python, for example, offers many data visualization libraries including Seaborn, Plotly, and Matplotlib that allow you to visualize data using Python commands inside your development environment. As a collection of pre-written code and standardized routines, libraries make executing advanced functions simple and easy. Sophisticated visualizations such as heatmaps and pairplots can be generated in just one line of code. The ability to generate visualizations inside a coding environment also helps with learning the makeup of your data and gaining feedback on the fly. In-line code visualizations, for example, provide feedback that you can use to inform your selection of algorithm hyperparameters.

To conclude, standalone software such as Tableau and Power BI is easy to learn and use, and they produce professional visualizations that you can easily share with end-users. The downside is that they come at a cost. Programming languages such as Python and R, combined with third-party libraries like Seaborn and Matplotlib, are a free alternative and extremely useful for the purpose of exploratory graphics.

## 13

BUSINESS INTELLIGENCE

While the public profile of prediction algorithms has enjoyed a meteoric rise in recent decades, few organizations have reached their peak in the internal development of god-like algorithms. Knocking elbows with DeepMind, Facebook, and IBM for new proprietary algorithms is well outside the remit of most companies and organizations. This isn't to say that other organizations shouldn't aspire to develop their own god-like algorithms, but that success isn't necessarily predicated on the development of one sublime algorithm.

In the car manufacturing industry, Toyota's ability to produce affordable and high-quality cars sits on the shoulders of its Total Production System (TPS) rather than one or two remarkable car designs. The Total Production System or Lean Manufacturing method is not a commercial secret—especially given there's an entire genre of literature detailing Toyota's methods. Toyota's unique advantage resides in its culture and ability to implement the system better than its competitors.

The same rules apply to data analytics. The algorithms are widely known and powerful techniques are available through the open-source community. But it all comes down to execution, and the integral steps before and after the algorithm are often overlooked. How well you clean your input data, for example, impacts your results—possibly even more than the algorithm itself. As machine learning instructor and former Amazon employee, Frank Kane, explains, "the inconvenient truth is you spend less time analyzing your data and more time preparing and cleaning" and not the other way around.[34] Datasets are also innately unique, which makes it difficult to transplant methods across organizations and replicate the same outcome.

Data scrubbing is only one rung in a shifting rope ladder of activity, and business intelligence relies on sensible decisions at each step. This includes choosing the variable types to collect (i.e. Boolean, numeric, categorical) and deciding what data is sent to the data warehouse for generating insight. Thus, sometimes the first algorithm to fine-tune is how your organization collects, prepares, and manages data internally.

The Business Intelligence Cycle

Business intelligence (BI) can be defined as a set of tools for gathering, analyzing, and reporting information to decision-makers regarding the organization's performance. By extracting data-driven insights about the organization, business intelligence empowers stakeholders to make superior business decisions.

Business decisions can be categorized into two overarching themes: *strategic decisions* and *operational decisions*. Strategic decisions determine the trajectory and direction of the company, including which products to manufacture and which customers to target. Operational decisions impact day-to-day workflow and internal efficiencies, such as hiring practices and product delivery management.

Predictive models can be developed to inform both types of decisions and revised over time as new data is fed back into the model. This ongoing practice of collecting and generating insight can give the organization a competitive advantage in the form of making better strategic decisions and reforming operational processes.[35] One university, for example, might employy

[34] Frank Kane, *Machine Learning, Data Science and Deep Learning with Python*, Sundog Education, Udemy.com.
[35] Anil Maheshwari, "Data Analytics Made Accessible," 2019 Edition.

clustering analysis to make decisions about alumni to target for requesting donations rather than mass-mailing its entire mailing list. New data can then help to validate or challenge the hypothesis established from the previous intake of data and turn the wheel for a new round of BI production.

While the intelligence or insight materializes at the end of the analysis, business intelligence isn't confined to the final reporting phase. It's diffused across multiple steps and each of the chapter topics covered in this book. Each step, from data collection, to data scrubbing, and deciding how the data is sorted or partitioned affects the output of business intelligence.

Given its ongoing and cyclical properties, business intelligence is typically described as a cycle and a quick Google image search returns an assortment of diagrams visualizing the BI cycle. While the sequencing and labels vary across diagrams and industries, the basic loop is to acquire data, mine insight, report findings, and take action. The cycle is eventually repeated by observing data from the outcome of actions (decisions) yielded from the previous cycle.

This constant feedback loop reflects how the organization is performing and has helped underwrite the growth of many successful data-driven companies including Amazon, Google, Netflix, Target, and Walmart.

Figure 33: Example of the business intelligence cycle

Without adequate and precise handling of data at each stage of the BI cycle, poor decisions can also go in circles and lead to bad outcomes. Simple mistakes like misreading correlation and causation can pre-empt poor business decisions, as we can see in Figure 34.

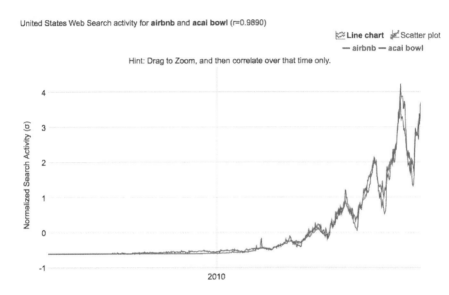

Figure 34: Google Correlate web search activity for airbnb and acai bowl

Using Google Correlate, we can see there's a high degree of correlation (0.9890) between Google searches for "airbnb" and "acai bowl" (a trendy Brazilian dish served as a smoothie). At first glance, Airbnb would be excused for thinking that people who search for their service are addicted to the acai bowl. With a correlation value nudging a maximum match value of 1.0, there's a strong case for Airbnb to open its own line of acai bowl stores in popular travel locations.

What's less clear is how this statistic and line chart were generated. In their frequently asked questions section, Google Correlate explains that their dataset comprises weekly updated web search activity data from January 2003 to the present. Thus, given the sheer volume of variables thrown at the search term "airbnb" for potential correlation, it's natural for one or more variables to resemble the original variable by coincidence rather than causation. Known as the *curse of dimensionality,* this problem tends to occur with new search terms whose patterns are less intricate. Conversely, Google is less likely to return a spurious match for well-established search terms like "Amazon" and "Starbucks."

Taking into account the vast number of variables directed at the target variable "airbnb" and the fact that Google Correlate doesn't filter for relevancy, we must be cognizant of potential mistruths and be vigilant about validating the results. In this case, more research (including guest surveys) and domain knowledge is needed to validate the relationship between Airbnb and the acai bowl before any further action is taken inside the BI cycle.

The second challenge to achieving BI nirvana is that not everyone is trained or inclined to play their part in the cycle. While data collection systems and metrics are more available than ever before, data-driven practices and skills might not penetrate key sections of the organization. If precise insight relies on the smooth running of each cog in the system, then the business intelligence cycle needs to be an enterprise-wide process and a culture of operating and not just a sphere of activity for data scientists.

An illustration of the right mindset can be seen in a memo issued by Amazon's CEO Jeff Bezos in the early 2000s, as paraphrased by a former employee.[36]

All teams will henceforth expose their data and functionality through **service interfaces**.

Teams must communicate with each other through these interfaces.

---

[36] Staci Kramer, "The Biggest Thing Amazon Got Right – The Platform," *Gigaom*, October 12 2011, https://gigaom.com/2011/10/12/419-the-biggest-thing-amazon-got-right-the-platform/

There will be no other form of interprocess communication allowed: no direct linking, no direct reads of another team's data store, no shared-memory model, no back-doors whatsoever. The only communication allowed is via service interface calls over the network.

It doesn't matter what technology they use. HTTP, Corba, Pubsub, custom protocols — doesn't matter.

All service interfaces, without exception, must be designed from the ground up to be externalizable. That is to say, the team must plan and design to be able to **expose** *the interface to developers in the outside world. No exceptions.*

Anyone who doesn't do this will be fired.

According to a number of commentators and former employees, this memo proved a key factor behind Amazon's success in the years following the Dotcom crash. The culture and direction embedded in this memo pushed Amazon to develop internal systems that would later be shipped to customers as revenue-generating API services. The deliberate direction prescribed by the memo forced developer teams to expose their data and consolidate common language protocols. By demanding data to be openly accessible both internally and externally, Bezos gave developers little space to hide. At the same time, it improved the overall efficiency and flexibility of Amazon's internal systems, including the universal service registry where relevant employees can find out about every service, its APIs, their running status, and where to find them.[37]

It's no accident that successful companies like Amazon promote a culture that values data-driven decisions. Establishing a mindset across an entire organization is difficult but setting an example at the top is a good place to start.[38] This includes emphasizing how

---

[37] Staci Kramer, "The Biggest Thing Amazon Got Right – The Platform," *Gigaom*, October 12 2011, https://gigaom.com/2011/10/12/419-the-biggest-thing-amazon-got-right-the-platform/

[38] "Why Your Company Culture is Key to Business Intelligence Success," *Phocas*

business intelligence is used as part of the overall business strategy and overturning monopolies and silos over who holds access to internal data. The default method of limiting access to decision-makers and executives in upper management oftentimes leads to poor practices at lower levels of the organization. It can also cause apathetic attitudes towards data among junior employees who work at the forefront of data collection. Rather than upload the company's webinar attendance data to the customer management system, the junior associate avoids this step because it seems secondary to their day-to-day work and key performance metrics. In addition, the employee probably doesn't have the expertise to visualize and analyze the data using software like Tableau. Conversely, when employees gain access and develop the expertise to filter and query business data to inform and enrich their work, it improves processes at all stages of the business intelligence cycle.

Data literacy at the top of the organization also helps to raise the bar for teams operating under their watch. Data expertise at the senior level makes it hard for junior employees to chisel at the truth, which tends to be rife in KPI-driven organizations.[39] An open data culture disincentivizes employees from presenting numbers that obscure or deviate from the truth (i.e. emphasizing the high open rate of an email campaign but hiding its low click-through rate), thanks to the threat of exposure and the full circumstances of the data being brought to light.

As a Gartner report on this topic duly notes, "The data can only take an organization so far. The real drivers are the people."[40]

Software, December 13 2016, https://www.phocassoftware.com/business-intelligence-blog/why-your-company-culture-is-key-to-business-intelligence-success
[39] In many organizations, key performance indicators (KPIs), bonuses, salary raises, and team budgets hinge on metrics generated by internal data.
[40] Elizabeth Dunlea, "The Key to Establishing a Data-Driven Culture," *Gartner*, November 30, 2015.

FROM THE AUTHOR

Knowledge of how data is collected, stored, manipulated, analyzed, and visualized is a crucial step toward gaining data literacy, and I hope this book brings you closer to driving the BI cycle in your organization.

If you have any direct feedback, both positive and negative, or suggestions to improve this book please feel free to drop me an email at **oliver.theobald@scatterplotpress.com**. This feedback is highly valued and I look forward to hearing from you.

You can also follow and find free learning materials and videos on my Instagram channel at **machinelearning_beginners**.

BUG BOUNTY

Thank you for purchasing this book. We offer a financial reward to readers for locating errors or bugs in this book. Some apparent errors could be mistakes made in interpreting a diagram or following along with the concepts introduced in the book, so we invite all readers to contact the author first for clarification and a possible reward, before posting a one-star review! Just send an email to **oliver.theobald@scatterplotpress.com** explaining the error or mistake you encountered.

This way, we can also supply further explanations and examples over email to calibrate your understanding, or in cases where you're right and we're wrong, we offer a monetary reward through PayPal or Amazon gift card. This way you can make a tidy profit from your feedback and we can update the book to improve the standard of content for future readers.

PRACTICAL DEMO: DESCRIPTIVE ANALYSIS

For readers that wish to get more hands-on with data analytics, this bonus chapter presents two coding examples that help to highlight the difference between descriptive and inferential techniques.

The practical examples covered in this chapter are coded using Python inside the Jupyter Notebook development environment. If you're new to computer programming or coding with Python, this chapter may prove challenging to comprehend on your first read. If so, rather than focusing on how Python commands are written and memorizing the code, I suggest focusing attention on what we're doing with the data and understanding the distinction between descriptive and inferential techniques.

This chapter is also complemented by video examples that walk you through how to install Jupyter Notebook and how to perform the necessary code presented in this chapter. You can find these videos at: **https://scatterplotpress.com/p/data-analytics**

About Python

Python was designed by Guido van Rossum during the late 1980s and early 1990s to empower developers to write programs with fewer lines of code than other languages. Python incorporates many English keywords (whereas other languages use punctuation) and has a reputation for being easy to learn.

Comments

In Python, comments can be added to your code using the # (hash) character. Everything placed after the hash character (on that line of code) is then ignored by the Python interpreter.

Variables

Variables are assigned in Python using the = operator.

Example:

```
dataset = 8
```

As mentioned in Chapter 3, variables in computer programming are slightly different from variables in statistics/data science. Rather than possessing a mathematical quality, variables in programming language refer to the storage of code. Similar to how you pack boxes labeled as "kitchen" and "garage" when moving house, variables act as a useful storage unit for data values or functions you want to use later. By calling the variable name in the future, you can task the Python interpreter to return your earlier code contained in that unique variable.

Python Data Types

Common data types in Python are shown in the following table.

Name	Explanation	Key Feature	Example
Integer	Whole numbers	No decimal point	50
Floating-point	Numbers with a decimal placing	Decimal point	50.1
String	Words and characters	Single/double quote marks	"Fifty5" or 'Fifty5'
List	Ordered sequence of objects	Square brackets	[1, 2, 3, 4, 'fifty']
Tuple	An order and immutable sequence of objects. Almost the same as a list, except values cannot be manipulated, thereby guaranteeing data integrity by preventing accidental changes in complex pieces of code.	Parenthesis	(1, 2, 3, 4)
Dictionary	Key-value pair. The key is denoted by a string such as a file name and linked to a value such as an image or text.	Curly brackets, colon, and quote marks	{"name" : "john", "gender" : "male"}
Set	An unordered collection of unique objects	Curly brackets	{"1", "2", "a"}
Booleans	Binary values	Capital initial (T/F)	**True** or **False**

Development Environment

For our development environment, we will be installing Jupyter Notebook, which is an open-source web application that allows for the editing and sharing of code notebooks. Jupyter Notebook can be installed using the Anaconda Distribution or Python's package manager, pip. As an experienced Python user, you may wish to install Jupyter Notebook via pip, and there are instructions available on the Jupyter Notebook website (http://jupyter.org/install.html) outlining this option. For beginners, I recommend choosing the Anaconda Distribution option, which offers an easy click-and-drag setup (https://www.anaconda.com/products/individual/).

This installation option will direct you to the Anaconda website. From there, you can select an Anaconda installer for Windows, macOS, or Linux. Again, you can find instructions available on the Anaconda website as per your choice of operating system.

After installing Anaconda to your machine, you'll have access to a range of data science applications including rstudio, Jupyter Notebook, and graphviz for data visualization. For this exercise, select Jupyter Notebook by clicking on "Launch" inside the Jupyter Notebook tab.

Practical Demonstration

In this first practical demonstration, we shall use descriptive methods to refine our understanding of the dataset. The dataset we are using contains information about restaurant tips provided by diners as shown below. Note that this is a snippet of the full dataset and the actual dataset has 244 rows (diners).

	total_bill	tip	sex	smoker	day	time	size
0	16.99	1.01	Female	No	Sun	Dinner	2
1	10.34	1.66	Male	No	Sun	Dinner	3
2	21.01	3.50	Male	No	Sun	Dinner	3
3	23.68	3.31	Male	No	Sun	Dinner	2
4	24.59	3.61	Female	No	Sun	Dinner	4

After installing Jupyter Notebook or an equivalent notebook, we need to import the necessary Python libraries. Libraries are a collection of pre-written code and standardized routines. Rather than write lines and lines of code in order to create a simple graph or scrape content from the web, you can use one line of code from a relevant library to run advanced functions.

The libraries used for this demonstration include Pandas, Seaborn, and Matplotlib.

Matplotlib is a visualization library you can use to generate scatterplots, histograms, pie charts, bar charts, error charts, and other visual charts using just a few lines of code. While Matplotlib offers detailed manual control over line styles, font properties, colors, axes, and properties, the default visual presentation is not as striking and professional as other visualization libraries and is often used in combination with Seaborn.

Seaborn is a popular Python visualization library based on Matplotlib. This library comes with numerous built-in themes for visualization and complex visual techniques including color visualization of dependent and independent variables, sophisticated heatmaps, cluster maps, and pairplots.

Pandas is an essential library for managing and presenting your data. The name "Pandas" comes from the term "panel data," which refers to Panda's ability to create a series of panels, similar to sheets in Excel. Pandas can be used to organize structured data as a *dataframe*, which is a two-dimensional data structure (tabular dataset) with labeled rows and columns, similar to a spreadsheet or SQL table. You can also use Pandas to import and manipulate an external dataset including CSV files as a dataframe without affecting the source file with modifications made inside your development environment.

```
# Import libraries
import pandas as pd
import seaborn as sns
import matplotlib.pyplot as plt
```

Next, we need to collect the dataset from https://raw.githubusercontent.com/mwaskom/seaborn-data/master/tips.csv using the **pd.read_csv** command from Pandas. Note that you'll also need to assign a variable name to store the dataset for ongoing reference, which in this case is df (short for 'dataframe').

```
# Import dataset
df = pd.read_csv("https://raw.githubusercontent.com/mwaskom/
seaborn-data/master/tips.csv")
```

This command directly imports the dataset into Jupyter Notebook.

Next, use the head() command to preview the dataset.

```
df.head()
```

Right-click and select "Run" or navigate from the Jupyter Notebook menu: Cell > Run All

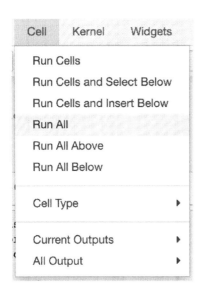

```
import pandas as pd
import seaborn as sns
import matplotlib.pyplot as plt

# Import dataset
df = pd.read_csv("https://raw.githubusercontent.com/mwaskom/seaborn-data/master/tips.csv")

df.head()
```

	total_bill	tip	sex	smoker	day	time	size
0	16.99	1.01	Female	No	Sun	Dinner	2
1	10.34	1.66	Male	No	Sun	Dinner	3
2	21.01	3.50	Male	No	Sun	Dinner	3
3	23.68	3.31	Male	No	Sun	Dinner	2
4	24.59	3.61	Female	No	Sun	Dinner	4

Note that the default number of rows displayed using the `head()` command is 5, but you can modify it by adding a number inside the parentheses, i.e. `head(10)`.

```
import pandas as pd
import seaborn as sns
import matplotlib.pyplot as plt

# Import dataset
df = pd.read_csv("https://raw.githubusercontent.com/mwaskom/seaborn-data/master/tips.csv")

df.head(10)
```

	total_bill	tip	sex	smoker	day	time	size
0	16.99	1.01	Female	No	Sun	Dinner	2
1	10.34	1.66	Male	No	Sun	Dinner	3
2	21.01	3.50	Male	No	Sun	Dinner	3
3	23.68	3.31	Male	No	Sun	Dinner	2
4	24.59	3.61	Female	No	Sun	Dinner	4
5	25.29	4.71	Male	No	Sun	Dinner	4
6	8.77	2.00	Male	No	Sun	Dinner	2
7	26.88	3.12	Male	No	Sun	Dinner	4
8	15.04	1.96	Male	No	Sun	Dinner	2
9	14.78	3.23	Male	No	Sun	Dinner	2

Task 1: How many days a week is the restaurant open?

Here, we can query the variable **day** and count the unique number of outcomes using the **len()** and **unique()** functions. The **len()** function counts the number of items in a data object, while **unique()** dictates that these items are unique/distinct.

```
len(df['day'].unique())
```

Right-click and select "Run" or navigate from the Jupyter Notebook menu: Cell > Run All

```
import pandas as pd
import seaborn as sns
import matplotlib.pyplot as plt

# Import dataset
df = pd.read_csv("https://raw.githubusercontent.com/mwaskom/seaborn-data/master/tips.csv")

len(df['day'].unique())
```
4

The answer for unique items contained in the variable **day** is 4 (Thursday, Friday, Saturday, and Sunday).

Task 2: Which day of the week has the most bills?

This time, we can use `value_counts()` to tally the total number of bills for each day based on the variable of **day**. We can then visualize the outcome using a count plot from Seaborn.

Note that rather than using `len()` and `unique()` to tally the unique number of items (i.e. Thur, Fri, Sat, Sun) for a given variable (as we did in the previous example), we are counting the total number of instances for each item (i.e. 100 bills on Thur).


```
df['day'].value_counts()
sns.countplot(data=df, x='day', order=['Thur', 'Fri',
'Sat', 'Sun'])
```

```
import pandas as pd
import seaborn as sns
import matplotlib.pyplot as plt

# Import dataset
df = pd.read_csv("https://raw.githubusercontent.com/mwaskom/seaborn-data/master/tips.csv")

df['day'].value_counts()
sns.countplot(data=df, x='day', order=['Thur', 'Fri', 'Sat', 'Sun'])
```

<matplotlib.axes._subplots.AxesSubplot at 0x1a1d4bd450>

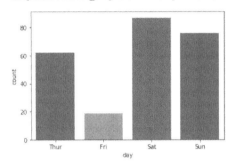

Here we can see that Saturday has the most bills and Friday has the least.

Task 3: Create heatmap

Lastly, let's create a heatmap in Python using the `corr` (correlation) function from Pandas and visualize the results using a Seaborn heatmap. Keep in mind that a heatmap only works with numerical/continuous variables, which for our dataset are the variables `total_bill`, `tip`, and `size`.

```
df_corr = df.corr()
sns.heatmap(df_corr,annot=True,cmap='coolwarm')
```

```
import pandas as pd
import seaborn as sns
import matplotlib.pyplot as plt

# Import dataset
df = pd.read_csv("https://raw.githubusercontent.com/mwaskom/seaborn-data/master/tips.csv")

df_corr = df.corr()
sns.heatmap(df_corr,annot=True,cmap='coolwarm')
```

<matplotlib.axes._subplots.AxesSubplot at 0x1a1d4b7350>

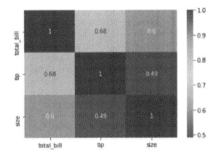

Based on the heatmap, we can see that the variables `tip` and `total_bill` have a higher correlation than other variable pairs, with a correlation score of 0.68. The variables `tip` and `size`, meanwhile, have a lower correlation score of 0.49.

PRACTICAL DEMO: INFERENTIAL ANALYSIS

For this second demonstration, we are going to use linear regression to predict what Mary will tip the restaurant based on the existing data.

The dependent variable (the variable we're aiming to predict) is `tip`, and the independent variables (that supposedly impact the dependent variable) are `total_bill`, `sex`, `smoker`, `day`, `time`, and, `size`.

1) Import Libraries

Different from the previous demonstration, we will be using an inferential approach in the form of linear regression. This means we need to import the linear regression algorithm from Scikit-learn, which offers an extensive repository of algorithms including logistic regression, decision trees, linear regression, gradient boosting, etc, plus a broad range of evaluation metrics and other methods.

```
# Import libraries
import pandas as pd
from sklearn.linear_model import LinearRegression
```

2) Import Dataset

As we did in the previous demonstration, we need to import the dataset into our work environment using Pandas and the `read_csv` command.

```
# Import dataset
df = pd.read_csv("https://raw.githubusercontent.com/mwaskom/
seaborn-data/master/tips.csv")
```

3) Convert Non-numeric Variables

Using one-hot encoding, let's convert each of the categorical features into numeric values using one-hot encoding.

```
# Convert variables sex, smoker, time and day to numerical
identifiers
df = pd.get_dummies(df, columns=['sex','smoker','time','day'])
```

Let's preview the transformation using `df.head()`

4) Set X and y Variables

Assign `tip` as the y target variable and the remaining variables as X.

```
# Assign X (independent) and y (dependent) variables
X = df.drop('tip',axis=1)
y = df['tip']
```

As seen in the code above, x contains all variables except 'tip' which has been dropped using the `drop` method.

5) Set Algorithm

Let's now assign the linear regression algorithm as a variable using the equals operator. The naming of the variable isn't important as long as it's an intuitive description and fits with Python's syntax for assigning variables (i.e. no spaces, cannot begin with a number, etc.). For this example, we will use `model` as the variable name.

```
# Assign algorithm as 'model'
model = LinearRegression()
```

Next, fit the model with the X and y variables.

```
# Link algorithm to the X and y variables
model.fit(X, y)
```

6) Predict

Let's now use the trained model to predict Mary's estimated tip. Mary is female, spends $10 for dinner on Friday, and is a non-smoker. Please also note that most of the variables below are binary (0 or 1). The first two variables, `size` and `total_bill` are continuous and non-binary, but all other variables are binary (1 = True or 0 = False).

```
# Input Mary's information (Female, $10, non-smoker, dinner
on Friday)
Mary = [
         10, #total_bill
         1, #size
         1, #sex_Female
         0, #sex_Male
         1, #smoker_No
         0, #smoker_Yes
         1, #time_Dinner
         0, #time_Lunch
         1, #day_Fri
         0, #day_Sat
         0, #day_Sun
         0, #day_Thur
]
```

Let's now use the `predict` function to execute the trained model using the variable `Mary` as new input data.

```
# Make prediction
Mary = model.predict([Mary])
Mary
```

To generate the model's prediction, we need to run the entire model by right-clicking and selecting "Run" or navigating from the Jupyter Notebook menu: Cell > Run All.

The results, as shown below, will then appear at the bottom of the notebook.

```
array([1.92467935])
```

```
# Input Mary's information (Female, $10, non-smoker, dinner on Friday)
Mary = [
    10, #total_bill
    1, #size
    1, #sex_Female
    0, #sex_Male
    1, #smoker_No
    0, #smoker_Yes
    1, #time_Dinner
    0, #time_Lunch
    1, #day_Fri
    0, #day_Sat
    0, #day_Sun
    0, #day_Thur
]

# Make prediction
Mary = model.predict([Mary])
Mary
```

```
array([1.92467935])
```

The predicted outcome is $1.92. We can't prove this outcome is absolutely true, but that's the very nature of inferential analysis. In reality, Mary is likely to round her tip up to $2, but using inferential analysis we can make an approximate prediction, which is useful for the restaurant to calculate and forecast future tips.

Summary

In the first demonstration, we used descriptive methods to tally variable items or values and visualized the correlation between continuous variables using a heatmap. In each example, we summarized known information about the data to derive insight that wasn't specifically labeled in the dataset.

In the second demonstration, we used linear regression as part of an inferential approach to make predictions based on historical data.

RECOMMENDED RESOURCES

Introduction to Advanced Analytics

Format: Whitepaper

Creator: Rapid Miner

This free whitepaper covers data mining, as well as predictive analytics, and business intelligence.

https://rapidminer.com/resource/introduction-advanced-analytics/

Data Mining For the Masses

Format: E-book

Creator: Rapid Miner

A free and comprehensive introduction to data mining.

https://rapidminer.com/resource/data-mining-masses/

Programming for Data Science

Format: Udacity course

A three-month online learning course with no technical skill prerequisites. This course involves 10 hours a week of coursework and is priced at USD $399 per month.

https://www.udacity.com/course/programming-for-data-science-nanodegree--nd104

Introduction to Data Analysis and Visualization

Creator: Mathworks

Format: Webinar

Introduction to data analysis and visualization using MATLAB.

https://www.mathworks.com/videos/matlab-tools-for-scientists-
introduction-to-data-analysis-and-visualization-81941.html

20 short tutorials all data scientists should read (and practice)

Creator: Data Science Central

A cheat sheet to resources for practical data science content.

http://www.datasciencecentral.com/profiles/blogs/17-short-tutorials-all-data-
scientists-should-read-and-practice

Machine Learning

Format: Free Coursera course

Presenter: Andrew Ng

A free and expert introduction from Adjunct Professor Andrew Ng, one of the most influential figures in this field. This course is a virtual rite of passage for anyone interested in machine learning. Suitable for beginners to machine learning with a general understanding of statistics and algorithms.

https://www.coursera.org/learn/machine-learning

Machine Learning for Absolute Beginners, Third Edition

Format: E-book, Book, Audiobook

Author: Oliver Theobald

Machine Learning for Absolute Beginners provides a clear and high-level introduction to machine learning including numerous algorithms and practical examples to help you build your first machine learning model.

Intro to Statistics

Format: Udacity course

As a free beginner's course to statistics on Udacity, this online resource introduces techniques for visualizing relationships in data and systematic techniques for understanding relationships using mathematics.

https://www.udacity.com/course/intro-to-statistics--st101

Linear Regression And Correlation: A Beginner's Guide

Format: E-book

Author: Scott Hartshorn

Suggested Audience: All

A well-explained and affordable (USD $3.20) introduction to linear regression and correlation.

The Power of Habit: Why We Do What We Do in Life and Business

Format: E-book, book, audiobook

Author: Charles Duhigg

While better classified under the self-help genre than machine learning, this book offers practical insight into human nature, which is relevant knowledge for data scientists. Chapter 7 (How Target Knows What You Want Before You Do) also includes one of the most detailed accounts of the famous Target marketing campaign that could discern if a customer was pregnant—even before the customer's father knew!

OTHER BOOKS BY THE AUTHOR

Machine Learning with Python for Beginners

Progress your Python skills by learning how to code machine learning models in Python and solve real-life problems.

Machine Learning for Absolute Beginners

Learn the fundamentals of machine learning, as explained in plain English.

Machine Learning: Make Your Own Recommender System

Learn how to make your own recommender system in an afternoon using Python.

Python for Absolute Beginners

Learn Python step-by-step to start building your first basic applications in an afternoon.

Statistics for Absolute Beginners

Master the fundamentals of inferential and descriptive statistics with a mix of practical demonstrations, visual examples, historical origins, and plain English explanations.

Made in the USA
Middletown, DE
27 May 2023

31554624R00092